Chasing Light

CHASING LIGHT

*Two Women, Their Mothers, and a Secret
That Changed Their Lives*

MAGGIE WRIGHT
TRACI MEDFORD-ROSOW

NEW YORK

LONDON • NASHVILLE • MELBOURNE • VANCOUVER • BOSTON

CHASING LIGHT

Two Women, Their Mothers, and a Secret That Changed Their Lives

Published in New York, New York, by Morgan James Publishing. Morgan James is a trademark of Morgan James, LLC. www.MorganJamesPublishing.com

Proudly distributed by Publishers Group West®

A **FREE** ebook edition is available for you
or a friend with the purchase of this print book.

CLEARLY SIGN YOUR NAME ABOVE

Instructions to claim your free ebook edition:
1. Visit MorganJamesBOGO.com
2. Sign your name CLEARLY in the space above
3. Complete the form and submit a photo
   of this entire page
4. You or your friend can download the ebook
   to your preferred device

ISBN 9781636988498 paperback
ISBN 9781636988504 ebook
Library of Congress Control Number:
2025941416

Cover Design by:
Morgan James Publishing

Interior Design by:
Chris Treccani
www.3dogcreative.net

Morgan James is a proud partner of Habitat for Humanity Peninsula
and Greater Williamsburg. Partners in building since 2006.

Get involved today! Visit: www.morgan-james-publishing.com/giving-back

Dedication

For our mothers and fathers

*"Two women, one broken and afraid,
the other broken and defiant.
As I turned to walk away, it occurred to me
that I did not know who was who."*

*—Unsheltered Love: Homelessness,
Hunger, and Hope in a City Under Siege*

Contents

Acknowledgments

First and foremost, I'd like to thank my co-author, Maggie Wright, without whom this book would not exist. To our beta readers—Joel Rosow, Carri Rubinstein, David Homick, Peter Richardson, and Maggie's mother—a special note of gratitude for your early and honest reflections. My editor and proofreader—Monique Conrod, your skill at catching all of those typos is inspiring. Last, but not least, I am grateful to the MJ publishing team.

Author's Note to Readers

In March 2020, my husband, Joel, and I were vacationing in Turks & Caicos. COVID-19 hit, the airport closed, and the world descended into chaos, confusion, and fear. We returned to our home in New York City on one of the last flights to leave the island.

While most of the residents had either fled the city for areas perceived to be safer, or were sheltering-in-place in their apartments, there was one group of residents still on the streets—the homeless men and women in our neighborhood. It quickly became apparent they were hungry. Empty streets translated into empty panhandling cups, resulting in empty stomachs.

We started making sandwiches, and for the remainder of 2020, we walked the deserted streets handing them out. During this period, we became acquainted with fifty or so homeless people, ten of whom appear in this book's prequel, *Unsheltered Love: Homelessness, Hunger, and Hope in a City Under Siege*. One of the people we met is Maggie Wright, who provided the journal excerpts in *Unsheltered Love*. She is also the co-author of this book.

This is a work of nonfiction. Some names have been changed for privacy, and some events are out of time sequence to aid the story's flow.

Prologue

"Success is to be measured not so much by the position that one has reached in life as by the obstacles which he has overcome."
—**Booker T. Washington**

Traci

As I look at Maggie rummaging through her school backpack, brow creased in focus, I am aware that I'm watching something extraordinary. Despite its mundane nature, this is no ordinary moment. It's a quiet, breathtaking miracle. However, it's not the type accompanied by a lot of public attention. There are no crowds or headlines. Rather, only a lucky few will ever know about it. I'm one of them.

When Maggie and I first met, the world was unraveling in the grip of a relentless pandemic. Maggie was homeless, and I was out on the deserted city streets handing out sandwiches. If someone had told me then that this same woman would one day find a home, much less return to college, I might have smiled politely and dismissed it as a beautiful but impossible dream.

And yet, here we are in her living room, Maggie packing up her backpack. Despite the darkness Maggie has endured, she is smiling, sunlight cascading across her face. Today, there is only light. Maggie has chased this light for many years, and so have I.

There are many ways I could have told this story. Only a year ago, I might have focused on the unlikely friendship between a homeless woman and an attorney. That would have been true but only part of the story. Now, there is only one story left to tell.

Ours is a story of mothers and daughters. Of intergenerational trauma passed down like heirlooms. Of trust broken, yet painfully rebuilt. More importantly, it's a story of healing. Of rising. Of bearing witness to the enduring light within us all.

This is our story of awakening.

PART ONE

Asleep

*"The great revelation perhaps never did come.
Instead, there were little daily miracles, illuminations,
matches struck unexpectedly in the dark"*
—Virginia Woolf

CHAPTER 1

Back to School

"The mind once enlightened cannot again become dark."
—**Thomas Paine**

Maggie

In January 2022, I went back to college. I was a forty-year-old homeless woman who'd dropped out of school twenty years earlier. On paper, I was just a statistic. But in my heart, I was also a mother, daughter, wife, sister, aunt, and author, quietly writing my story under the pen name Maggie Wright. The pseudonym was a fragile shield, protecting my children from a world I never imagined I'd have to survive.

This is the story of that world. It's also the story of meeting one woman who helped me crawl out of it, and who, despite her outward appearance and circumstances, was in a battle of her own.

We met by chance. Or maybe it was fate. It was a cold, foreboding March morning, the kind that seeps into your bones. The world was quieted by a global pandemic, hushed and hollow. The streets were empty. But I was still on them because I had no place else to go. And for some inexplicable reason, a woman named Traci was on them too.

Two years later, the pandemic almost behind us, I sat in the back row of my classroom, shoulders hunched, heart pounding, waiting for the professor to enter. A few minutes later, an elderly woman bumbled in, disheveled in a charming Columbo kind of way, papers spilling from her briefcase. She smiled and looked directly at me, allaying my concerns somewhat. *Was she wondering what a middle-aged woman was doing in her class? Did she somehow know I was homeless?* She introduced herself as Professor Barrett and then asked each of us to say a few words about ourselves.

My stomach twisted. I didn't know whether I should tell the truth or make up some story about a midlife "awakening." I was grateful to be in the back row. It gave me some extra time to collect my thoughts, even if it also gave me enough time to spiral. I gripped the edges of my desk, my palms slick with sweat.

When it was my turn to speak, I steadied my nerves and took a deep breath. "My name is Maggie. I'm a formerly homeless woman. For the past eighteen months, I've been able to live with my boyfriend, William, in public housing. I was homeless for four years, and for three of those years, I slept on the sidewalk in Manhattan. Twenty years ago, I dropped out of college when I failed my statistics final, but I'm back now to finish my degree."

An uneasy silence permeated the room. Thick. Heavy. I wasn't sure if it was coming from the teacher, the students, me, or all of us. It didn't matter. I wanted to run. I did not belong in a college classroom. *Who was I kidding?* My place was on the streets with my girlfriends and William.

William lived in an old brownstone-type building on Snediker Avenue in Brooklyn. It was a two-bedroom apartment that had been converted into a three-bedroom by erecting a temporary wall in part of the living room. Technically, only three men were supposed to live there, but the caseworker looked the other way when I and another woman moved in and shared the bedrooms assigned to our boyfriends.

One of our roommates, Paul, was kind, gentle, and wise in a way that only age and hardship can teach. But the other man and his girlfriend were lost and desperate, addicted to crack. She prostituted herself to make money, and more than one unsavory character found his way into the apartment.

William and I both smoked weed, and we were not averse to a cheap bottle of vodka, either, but we did not use hard drugs. Nor did Paul. In order to escape the ugly scene in our apartment as often as possible, William and I roamed the streets, every day, all day. William sold five-dollar K2 blunts, a synthetic form of weed, to make a little extra cash for us. Selling blunts was not without its risks, however. William got into more than one turf war with other homeless men over who could sell blunts on which city blocks.

Even though our housing was free, and William and I each received cash assistance (I got $123 twice a month; William got $91—less than me because he was officially housed) and monthly food stamps (we each received $275), it was not enough to cover all our expenses.

We'd adopted a stray Chihuahua named Georgia that our neighbors had dumped on the street one December morning during the pandemic because they could no longer afford to feed her. She quickly became the light of our lives. However, her food and vet bills were not insignificant. There were many times when William and I went hungry to make sure we could pay for Georgia's food. We'd also adopted a stray kitten we named Tyson, a mischievous little thing with soft fur, who likewise filled our hearts with love. Tyson's food, kitty litter, and other supplies also mounted up.

I looked around my classroom. There did not appear to be any other homeless people. In fact, no other student appeared older than twenty-something. I felt out of place and found myself daydreaming about a recent afternoon I'd spent on the sidewalk with my three girlfriends—Melissa, Knicki, and Della—a heroin addict, a professional thief, a prostitute, and me, the homeless college dropout.

We could have been any four women sitting around a living room. We enjoyed the sunshine, each of us with our own tub of ice cream, engaged in meaningless, but ever-so-interesting, girl talk. I'd felt far more comfortable in that situation than my classroom.

After class, I gathered up my books and papers and bolted out the door. Suddenly, I felt a light tap on my right shoulder. It was another student, a well-dressed young woman who appeared to have her life together.

"Excuse me, my name is Kristen. I hope this isn't rude, but would you mind telling me how you became homeless." She looked nervous, yet, at the same time, determined. "My sister, Pam, has disappeared, and my family fears the worst," she said, holding out her phone to show me a picture of her sister.

I glanced at the picture. She looked familiar. Many homeless people either know each other or know of each other. "Is she an addict?" I asked bluntly.

Kristen's eyes widened. "How did you know?"

"Most homeless people are—or, at least, were. Addiction does not discriminate. It barges in, unannounced and uninvited. Rich, poor, young, old, white, Black, or brown, it does not care who its next victim will be."

Kristen lowered her head. "Pam is addicted to painkillers. She's an athlete—tore her ACL playing soccer in college."

I studied the photo again. I thought it might be a woman Traci knew whose name was Jen. "Can you send me a screenshot of that picture, please? And do you have time to grab a cup of coffee? I may know where your sister panhandles. And while we drink our coffee, I'll tell you the short version of how I became homeless. You won't be surprised to learn, it was also the result of painkillers."

Kristen grabbed my hand. "Let's go. I have all the time you need."

◆ ◆ ◆

My story of homelessness began in 2016 when I lost not only my home, but myself. I was living in New Jersey with my husband, his parents, and our two young children. I had an office job at a nearby nursery school. Life wasn't perfect, but I was safe.

Then one morning, I woke up and couldn't talk. Tooth on fire. A trip to the dentist seemed to be the proper course of action. Back then, I had good dental and medical insurance. I needed a root canal—my first—and I needed it quickly.

The next day, I was taking the opioid prescription the dentist had given me for the pain. So far, so good. Then I developed a dry socket, and he gave me another five-day supply of those little white pills that not only took away the throbbing pain in my mouth, but also the less-defined, deeper, throbbing I hadn't even realized was there.

By the time both prescriptions ran out, I was already hooked. The first day without meds was tough. The second, horrible. I was at work and went into my boss's office to ask if I could go home early. I told her I'd run out of meds and my mouth was still killing me. She went into her bag and gave me a handful of pills, as if they were candy, and told me to let her know if I needed more. I was flabbergasted. My boss was the director of a private nursery school.

Thus began my addiction to pain pills. My boss, it turned out, was also addicted to those pills, and her husband dealt them. Now, we were in this together, and she paid me for overtime work with pills.

Most people can take their prescription of opioids and be fine. But some of us—the unlucky ones like me—it's a chemical battle from the first pills that register in our brains. I didn't realize this until many years later when I saw the Netflix series *Painkiller*. Bone-chilling, to say the least, it described exactly how the opioid crisis in America began, and then thrived, claiming thousands of lives, including mine.

My addiction escalated. Soon, I was buying 120 pills from cancer patients at the beginning of the month for $1200 a bottle. One hundred and twenty pills became 180. By the summer of 2016, I could no longer afford the pills and decided to quit. Locking myself away in my bedroom, I suffered in silence. The withdrawal felt like the worst flu I'd ever experienced. On the third day, I decided to take a shot of vodka. After the shot, I felt a bit better, so I took another one.

A few months later, I'd broken my opioid addiction, but I'd become a full-blown alcoholic. Things deteriorated rapidly. That Christmas, my husband and I flew to Florida with our children to visit my parents, who, despite being separated at that point, had remained friends and lived in separate apartments in the same retirement community.

The trip was a nightmare. I drank every bottle of alcohol in my father's liquor cabinet, and one night, while he was sleeping, I took his credit card and paid the $780 fine that was keeping an old boyfriend in jail. He was free, but I had just erected another bar in my own prison cell.

We returned to New Jersey, and I went back to work. Within a few weeks, however, I was no longer able to function properly. My boss helped by laying me off without cause instead of firing me, and I went on unemployment. For the first time since I was a teenager, I didn't have a job.

I offered to do carpool to school in the morning so someone else would drive in the afternoon. A full-blown alcoholic, I still had enough sense to make sure my children were safe. With no job and the kids in school, the days were boring. My drinking escalated.

No one could stand being around me. I couldn't even stand being around myself. My mother-in-law "suggested" everyone would be better off if I moved out and got my own apartment until I could get myself together. I have to admit, it seemed like a good idea at the time, even though my children were young. They deserved better than to be around a broken mother. In any event, I thought I'd be back soon.

With some money I still had from our tax refund, I stayed in a hotel for a week. From there, I moved to a motel efficiency apartment. With financial help from my parents, I settled into my new life.

That was the first time I'd lived on my own. The first few weeks were fine. I picked up an easy day job at a local deli and attended the kids' sports games in the evenings. Afterward, I'd go home, drink a bottle of vodka, and pass out. Over time, I became lonely because most of my friends were also my husband's, which made things awkward.

I asked for permission to go back home. The request was denied. I asked my husband to move in with me, but he declined as well. I can't blame him, and not just because I was an alcoholic. We were very good friends and never fought, but there was no passion in our marriage. Most nights, I went to sleep while he played on the computer, and while we coexisted peacefully, I wouldn't call it a love story. Looking back, he must have been as uninterested in me as I was with him. We were just two people who coexisted, tethered together by habit and the fragile lives of our two young children.

Nevertheless, despite the boredom, we'd enjoyed a decent life together, and I am not blaming my husband for what happened. Living alone in the motel apartment, I soon regretted having taken my boring life for granted. I missed it all.

I'd been a member of the mothers' league and was class mother for both my kids' classes. I went on field trips, baked cookies, and drove carpools. Most weekends and afternoons were filled with activities for the kids—soccer, cheerleading, swimming, and gymnastics for my daughter. T-Ball, soccer, Ninja Warrior classes, and hockey for my son. I drove an SUV and gained a lot of weight—topping off at 225 pounds. But I was safe, and I was loved. I often complained that I was "just a mother." Oh, how I wish I could say those three words now.

My husband and I had met in an online chat room. He was different from any other man I'd dated. For one, he'd earned a 1590 on his SAT. He was also a virgin, four years younger than I was, a social outcast, and had never so much as liked a girl, let alone had a girlfriend.

He played *Dungeons and Dragons*. I played *World of Warcraft*—an online role-playing game set within a fantasy universe. He soon joined me in our alternate world, and we would talk for hours through our headsets while we played. We made an excellent team in the game, and we had a lot in common when it came to books, movies, and politics.

After a year of playing online, we decided to meet in person, and things progressed from an online relationship to a long-distance one. He lived in New Jersey, and I in Brooklyn, New York. We both had jobs and worked during the week and saw each other on the weekends. It was no great love affair—just a friendship with sexual benefits that led to our greatest blessing. Our daughter arrived the following spring, healthy and beautiful, promising us a new life.

Two children and many years later, my husband still lived with his parents, and I was in a dark and damp motel efficiency apartment, a few miles away. But we were beginning to patch things up a bit until life threw me another curveball.

I paused long enough to notice Kristen was crying. A mixture of shame and guilt overwhelmed me. "Maybe we should pick this up next week after class?" I suggested. "It seems you've heard enough of my story for one day."

"That's probably a good idea," Kristen replied, wiping her eyes.

CHAPTER 2

A Friend Request

"Education breeds confidence.
Confidence breeds hope. Hope breeds peace."
--Confucius

Maggie

The following week after class, Kristen grabbed my arm with an intensity that surprised me.

"Will you please finish telling me how you became homeless?" she asked.

"Sure, if you really want me to. It's not a pretty story though, and I don't want to upset you."

"Forget the coffee," Kristen suggested. "Let's get a beer."

◆ ● ◆

One night, feeling sorry for myself in that lonely hotel efficiency, I was getting drunk and browsing Facebook when a friend-request notification popped up. It was from my cousin Rick who'd been missing for eight years. It was as if he'd literally disappeared off the planet, and no one in the family knew where he was. Even his father didn't have any information.

Rick was older than I was. Our fathers were first cousins—which made us second cousins—and we'd known each other since childhood. Probably as a result of our age difference, but also because Rick had always been intelligent and charismatic, I looked up to him.

Rick's father, a prominent dentist, had been a little bit embarrassed by Rick because he was the result of an affair he'd had with his Hispanic dental assistant. Rick's mother had primary custody, but Rick spent every other weekend with his father.

When we were young, Rick and I were very close, so I was thrilled to hear from him. He was living in Manhattan in a transitional living facility for homeless people. I couldn't believe it. My handsome, intelligent, and charming cousin was homeless! My first, second, and third instincts were to help him.

I messaged him immediately and gave him an abbreviated version of the recent events in my life. He told me he would love to see me, and I offered to pick him up the following day and bring him to New Jersey for the weekend. Rick's sudden appearance felt like destiny. Like hope.

The following evening, I drove into the city. It rained the whole way, water splashing off my headlights like broken glass. I pulled up in front of his shelter. Rick was waiting outside, despite the rain. Flashing his mischievous smile, he jumped into the passenger seat before the car had come to a complete stop.

We spent the ride back to New Jersey catching up on the past few years. He told me a bit about his life, and I was horrified. Of course, I had no idea the same fate awaited me.

When we got back to my apartment, Rick asked if I wanted to smoke. My husband and I had smoked a little weed over the years, but I'd not had any for a while. Rick pulled out a blunt. It was the best stuff I'd ever had.

Rick laughed. The joke was on me. It wasn't weed I'd just enjoyed. It was a "woolie," which is a mixture of crack cocaine and K2. I'd never heard of K2 and was momentarily horrified that I'd just been given two drugs that I'd never used before. An opioid addiction had been bad enough! That moment quickly passed, however, and I asked for another pull. Another one of my less than brilliant moves.

Before I knew it, Rick was spending most of his time in New Jersey. We drove back to New York every three days so he could sign in at his building. It's probably hard to believe, but the only requirement of homeless people living in transitional housing is to show up once every three days to sign the clipboard. They are not even required to spend the night! Something is wrong with that rule when there are so many people sleeping on the streets, but that's for the system to figure out.

The drive back and forth to the city was expensive and exhausting, but I loved Rick's company and the drugs. I was drinking less and smoking more. A second addiction was giving way to a third. I fell in love with K2. It was like weed on steroids, but it made my brain calm, the omnipresent chaos silenced. I felt like I could see and think clearly, as opposed to the hazy and forgetful feeling I experienced from booze.

The first few weeks, we had a great time, and I was thrilled to have Rick back in my life. I even took him to see my kids play soccer one night. I thought my life was coming back into focus, literally and figuratively. However, I was about to find out that my cousin had a dark side to his personality I'd never seen when we were young.

Rick's bad behavior escalated and the motel efficiency became dirtier and smaller by the day. One night, Rick started punching holes in the wall.

The next morning, the landlord showed up and inspected the apartment. He gave me one week to find another place. I went to the motel next door and spoke with the woman who ran it. She was in need of a housekeeper, and I was in need of a place to live. We came to an agreement. The following week, I moved into a tiny efficiency in her motel in exchange for cleaning services. No pay. No dignity. Just survival.

A month later, Rick decided he no longer wanted to go back to New York, preferring to live in New Jersey full-time. Rick lost his room, and things soon went from bad to worse. He became moody and resentful because we didn't have any money. I'd had to give up my job at the deli in order to have time to clean the motel rooms, and Rick couldn't collect money panhandling in New Jersey like he did in Manhattan. He grew sullen, then angry, then violent.

One night we had a fight, and Rick broke all the lamps and shattered the window. The next morning, the police knocked on the door. Once again, I had to pack my things and leave.

Out of options, I called the only friend I had left in New Jersey—my son's best friend's mother, Stella. I explained the situation, and she invited us to move into her house. For six precious weeks, we managed to live together peacefully. Six weeks of false hope. Six weeks of pretending that everything was okay. Then one night, true to form, Rick got drunk and picked a fight.

The next morning, Stella tiptoed into the living room before the sun came up and motioned for me to follow her into the laundry room. I knew what it was about. How could she not have heard the yelling in the middle of the night? Rick's screaming had scared her children. Stella handed me fifty dollars, and I knew what it meant. I had to leave her house. Immediately. Her children were hiding in their rooms, too afraid to come downstairs for breakfast. Shame of shames!

We'd lasted there longer than in either motel efficiency. Stella had graciously taken us in. She'd opened her home, and her heart, and her fridge. We had no money and nothing to offer her, but she took us in, anyway. Now, I stood in the middle of her living room, fifty-dollar bill in hand, officially homeless. No address. No illusions.

◆ ◆ ◆

Again, I noticed Kristen's tears. "Let's stop for today," I suggested, putting down my beer. "In the meantime, I will call my friend Traci and ask her if she recognizes your sister and knows where she is."

"Why would your friend know my sister? Is she homeless too?"

"That's another long story," I replied.

CHAPTER 3

Empty Streets

*"Do your little bit of good where you are; it's those little bits of
good put together that overwhelm the world."*
—Desmond Tutu

Traci

As soon as Maggie left Kristen, she called me. "Hey. I just sent you a picture of a young girl. Do you by any chance recognize her?"

I looked at my phone. I was sure I recognized her. I searched through the photo album on my phone—the one I'd named "homelessness"—to see if I also had a photo of same girl. I had hundreds of pictures of the homeless men and women I'd befriended during the pandemic. And there she was. Her name was Jen.

◆ ◆ ◆

I remember the exact day I first saw Jen—March 22, 2020. Joel and I had been back in the city for four days, having abruptly returned from the Caribbean due to the pandemic.

19

That morning, I went for a long walk because there was little else to do. I was alone. On the way home, I stopped at the deli on the corner of 34th and Park to pick up some food. A young and attractive girl was panhandling outside. I dropped my change into her tattered cup.

At first glance, she did not appear homeless. However, her dirty hands and panhandling cup revealed the truth. As I started to walk toward my apartment, I paused and turned around. *How was it possible that this young girl was homeless?*

It had only been a few days since Governor Cuomo's official "pause" order had been issued, yet the transformation in the city was already profound. I don't think I'm exaggerating when I say one of the most vibrant cities in the world, once alive with the pounding rhythm of millions of lives, resembled a war-ravaged ghost town. Stores were closed, doors were bolted, lights were out. The sidewalks, the veins of human connection, were empty. An eerie silence whistled through the shuttered windows, revealing the emptiness of the rooms they hid.

Despite the silence, the city moaned quietly under the weight of grief and fear. The death toll mounted at a rapid rate. By March 18, over 3000 cases of coronavirus had been reported, 463 people had been hospitalized, and 20 had died.

That day—the day I first saw Jen—was my grandmother's birthday. She would have been 119 years old that year, and even though she had long since passed, I still thought about her often. Especially on her birthday. Mary Tully McCormick, née Birney, was Irish, with fire-engine red hair and a will and temper to match. If anyone pissed her off, she'd let them know it in no uncertain terms. But with me, well, I only saw the good side of her.

To be honest, however, there was *one* time I saw that other side. My cousin Bobby made the mistake of using the N-word in her presence, an absolute no-no in our family. The next thing I knew, Bobby had a bar of soap in his mouth and was sitting in the corner, nose toward the wall. From that day forward, he never used that word again. He also took to calling my mother's cleaning lady *ma'am* and her husband *sir,* just for good measure.

That day marked the first time it came into my conscious awareness that many of the homeless people of New York City were starving. Empty streets translated into empty panhandling cups, which resulted in empty stomachs. No stray kindness. Just gnawing, endless hunger.

I looked up and down what only days before had been one of the busiest streets in the world, now empty of life. No people, no dogs, and not a single car. Park Avenue, one of the nicest streets in Manhattan, is also the widest, with several lanes of traffic running in both directions. A combination of residential buildings and retail spaces border the wide, tree-lined boulevard, which resembles the streets of Paris. I had never seen it empty before, even in the middle of the night. But that day there were no honking cars, rushing feet, or barking dogs, just an eerie silence.

I shivered in the cold, looking for some sign of life. Anything. A person, a sound, a light. Literally, out of the blue, a lone seagull searching for food flew overhead, an abnormal screeching sound piercing the morning silence, drawing my attention upward toward the blue sky. I've often marveled at the seagulls flying over the city. Their presence is due to the two rivers on either side of the island—the East River and the Hudson River—both of which are brackish.

That morning, I did not recognize the screeching sound but would come to know it all too well in the following weeks and months. A raw, animal plea.

That bird was hungry, as were the squirrels I'd seen in the empty Madison Square Park the day before. As I'd sat on an empty park bench eating a sandwich, a squirrel approached and sat at my feet, hands seeming to form a prayer. *Was it asking for food?* It looked directly at me and did not move. I tore off a piece of my sandwich and offered it, my hand shaking in fear of being bitten as well as from the realization that I was alone in the park.

Even though the animals in New York City are not domesticated, they are not exactly wild, either. They depend on the food droppings of thousands of city residents who eat while they walk to work, dine outside, and otherwise intentionally leave half-eaten sandwiches around for the pigeons. But there was no one walking to work that morning.

Hunger is not only a condition that makes people uncomfortable and thin. It's an odor that is unmistakable, clinging to its victims like a shadow. It's not just bad breath from an empty stomach. It more closely resembles the smell of death.

As I left the deli with two fresh muffins, my stomach grumbled. But, unlike Jen, I had a full refrigerator. I had money. It occurred to me that while my colleagues and I were able to continue working remotely, so many vulnerable citizens were cut off from any possibility of making a living—restaurant workers, hair stylists, manicurists, gig workers, and also panhandlers—people who did not earn a salary, but rather were paid by the job, the hour, the tip, the handout. Nevertheless, I told myself there was not much I could do to help. Especially now. Especially in the middle of a raging pandemic. Yet deep in my gut, I knew this wasn't true.

The nagging in my stomach that morning was more than hunger. I knew I had two options—stay in my apartment until the virus was over, or get out on the streets and help the homeless in whatever small or big ways I could. The decision was binary. I knew the answer before I'd even asked myself the question. I had to be able to look in the mirror when the nightmare was over.

The irony of that morning was that I wasn't supposed to be walking the streets. Shelter-in-place, although not an official law, was a clearly defined, unwritten rule. Governor Cuomo had decreed that residents should only leave their homes to buy food or medical supplies, or in the worst-case scenarios, seek medical help.

But there was one exception—we were allowed to go outside to exercise. I dove headfirst into that "loophole" and never looked back. Why I did it is a question I've been asked hundreds of times. I still do not know the answer, but I suspect it had something to do with my mother, Jean Tully Medford, and her addiction to Valium. Sadly, it was my very existence that had caused it.

◆◆◆

I was born in June 1955 in the still small, but burgeoning, city of Alexandria, Virginia. As I entered the world, one of the vertebrae in my mother's lower spine shattered. A chain reaction was set in motion that would change the course of her life, as well as mine. The pain that began in my mother's spine would seep into every corner of our home, creating darkness, stillness, and carefully-guarded secrets.

Jean Tully Medford was a college-educated, athletic beauty. My father, Charles Medford, often reminded me how unusual it was for a woman to have a college degree in 1950. My mother attended George Washington University on a basketball scholarship. At the time, my father was two hours away at the University of Virginia, a college student himself, thanks to the GI bill.

Their story began with a blind date. One of my father's fraternity brothers set him up with his girlfriend's best friend, who happened to be my mother. For their remaining two years of college, my parents carried on a long-distance relationship that apparently worked. Following their graduations in 1950, they were married. Five years later, I was born.

After my birth, the doctor prescribed Valium to manage my mother's pain, and, like Maggie, I suspect she was unlucky and whatever momentary relief the pills offered quickly turned into dependence, and dependence into addiction. Jean Tully Medford's descent into darkness officially began at the age of twenty-six.

I didn't realize that my mother was an addict until my teenage years, and even then, it was not clearly in focus. But what I did know was that something was wrong in our house—a sort of quiet and darkness that enveloped us. The more we tried to hide it, the more solid it became behind our closed doors and curtain-covered windows.

I wonder now how many of our neighbors knew the truth. My mother was quite a lady and could put on a good front. The identical split-level houses in our neighborhood were set on one-third-acre parcels, so there was not much distance between them. However, there was not a lot of screaming going on in our house; rather, it was the silence and the absence of my mother that became the most deafening. In fact, I have very few memories of my mother during my elementary school years. Two, to be precise.

The first is when my younger brother, Jeff, and I returned from school one day. I was nine and Jeff was six. Our mother was waiting for us on the front porch with lemonade and cookies that she'd just made. My heart leapt with joy, and we both ran toward her as she stood in the sunshine—her bathrobe and light-brown hair billowing in the spring breeze—smiling and waving. *Yes! Our mother was out of bed and in a good mood!*

The second memory is when I was in fifth grade. One morning before school, I found my mother downstairs in our den, polishing the furniture. I wandered too close to the table, and she said, "Move your little leg." Just that. But it was enough. In that moment, I knew my mother loved me because she did not want something to fall off the table and hurt my leg.

That was a special moment for me because my mother did not say the words "I love you" often. In fact, I only remember her saying those three words to me once. It was the last time I spoke to her, and it was the very last thing she said before we hung up the phone. I should have known something was wrong, but I didn't. Or if I did, I have no conscious memory of it. I was twenty-three years old and still self-absorbed.

There is one other thing I remember well. To this day, every moment is still vivid, even though at the time I did not think much of it. I was home from college on Christmas break. I found my mother downstairs in our finished, above-ground basement. She was drinking, although this was not her main problem.

I surprised her. And for some reason, I asked a question. "Why do you love Jeff more than me?" Nonplussed, she replied, "It's natural to root for the underdog." I didn't cry. I didn't argue. I shrugged and went about my business, accepting her reply like I'd accepted her absence.

What I remember most about my mother is the empty space she left behind. I don't remember a single activity we did together. No shopping trips, no lunches, no one-on-one girl time, no walks. I don't even remember having a conversation with her.

Rather, it was my grandmother who raised me. Every day after school, I walked to her house and we'd spend the afternoons together. Usually, we sewed. My grandmother was a gifted seamstress, and I was happy to help her with whatever she was making that day. Her presence was like a soft quilt—warm, dependable, stitched together with patience and love.

Sometimes I would gather pine needles from the woods surrounding my grandparents' house. My grandfather paid me ten cents for each wheelbarrow load. "Pack 'em down tight, Sam," my grandfather would admonish, using the nickname he'd given me. "I'm not paying for any half loads."

This posed one of the first conundrums I had to solve as a young child. No matter how slowly I walked, by the time I got the wheelbarrow back to my grandfather's garden, it appeared to be only partially full. I finally figured out a trick. I stored a huge pile of needles at the edge of the woods, and when I reached it, I'd refresh my wheelbarrow so that it was full when I arrived at my grandfather's garden. Those dimes were important to me, providing a means to buy candy at the nearby deli.

My grandfather used those needles for mulch in his garden, a vibrant array of fruits and vegetables that our family ate all year long. Not a scrap was wasted. We filled our bellies from spring through fall, and then we also had an assortment of just about everything stored in canning jars in my grandmother's basement for the short winters.

As much as I liked those dimes, I would have been happy to gather the pine needles free of charge. Surrounded by trees, I was in my happy place. I could escape from everybody and everything in those woods. An expansive paradise, there was always another place to explore. Among the trees, I could breathe. I could forget. No one yet worried about children being abducted, so I was able to roam freely for hours.

My father did his best to keep the household running. My grandmother and aunt were too upset to face the truth. We all carried pieces from my mother's unraveling, but no one spoke about it aloud.

Despite the undeniable evidence, it wasn't until I watched the 2022 Netflix show *Take Your Pills: Xanax,* almost a half century after her death, that I finally understood what my mother's addiction had done to her. I also understood that my mother was a victim of Valium, a benzodiazepine similar in structure to Xanax. Both Valium and opioids have destroyed hundreds of thousands of lives, including my mother's. I also understood that an addict does not just destroy his or her life, but the lives of many people around them.

However, what I had not yet understood was how deeply broken I was. But when I started walking the empty streets of New York City and saw the haunted eyes of the homeless, something inside me awakened. I saw myself in them—the same secrets, the same struggle, the same searching.

The pain I'd buried so long ago was still there, hidden behind layers of survival and silence. It had lived inside me, waiting for the moment when I'd finally stop running away from it. To stop chasing the next achievement, the next quick fix, the next distraction. It wanted my attention. It wanted me to listen.

CHAPTER 4

Beaches and Ferris Wheels

"One day, in retrospect, the years of struggle
will strike you as the most beautiful."
—Sigmund Freud

Maggie

The following week, I forced myself to go to class, determined to speak with Kristen about Jen. I had a few pictures, which Traci had found in her photo album, and I wanted to show them to her. It's not unusual for homeless people to change their names. Even William went by his nickname, Civil.

After class, I motioned to Kristen to follow me out into the hall. I opened the photos on my phone and showed her the pictures. "Is this your sister?"

Kristen gasped. "Yes, that's Pam! Do you know where she is?"

"This girl goes by the name of Jen," I said. "Are you sure it's Pam?"

"Yes, I'm certain. Pam's name is Pamela Jennifer Stuart."

"I don't know where she lives—or if she even has a room—but I do know where Traci took these pictures. It was on the corner of Park Avenue and 34th Street, outside of the deli."

"Can you send these pictures to me, please?" Kristen asked.

"Of course. Traci lives four blocks away and sees Jen panhandling on the corner. She said to feel free to call her, and she will arrange to go with you to look for your sister. I'll text you Traci's number."

The next day, Traci called. "I just spoke to Kristen. She's coming to my apartment this afternoon, and we will walk down to the deli together."

Despite growing closer to Kristen, I continued to struggle to make it to class. The commute from my apartment to school was an hour. But I don't think that was the root cause of my difficulty. I just felt out of place in that classroom. The workload was not hard, but socially, I felt awkward.

Interestingly, I had no problem with my online class on Zoom. Perhaps the anonymity of seeing my classmates in little squares on my laptop provided enough emotional distance to ensure my comfort. But that in-person class was a different story. It felt like being under a spotlight with no script.

I was only allowed two unexcused absences, and I used one the following week and the second one a few weeks later. Faced with the possibility of flunking the class, I dropped it halfway through the semester. Relief flooded in as soon as I hit the "drop class" button on my laptop. That feeling lasted for five minutes. Then panic set in. *What was I going to tell Traci?*

I knew she would eventually find out when it was time to register for the summer session. She paid for my tuition through her private foundation. However, a condition precedent for obtaining additional tuition assistance was that I complete my first two classes with a B average. That was now impossible.

I sat at my desk in my apartment on Snediker Avenue, staring out the window. I felt hollow and defeated. Even after all these years, my uncanny ability to self-destruct surprised even me. I could only imagine what Traci would have to say when she found out what I'd done now. I'd come so far since the day Rick and I had arrived in New York City four years earlier, and now, I'd blown it. Again.

I tried to comfort myself by remembering that first day I'd become homeless. A dropped college class paled into insignificance. I could figure it out.

◆ ◆ ◆

Standing in Stella's living room, fear began to overwhelm me. Where would we go? How would we survive? Where would we sleep that night? For the first time in my life, I had nowhere to go and no one to turn to for help.

I don't think I've ever felt as lonely, defeated, and disappointed as I did in that moment. I remember going into the bathroom after Stella handed me that fifty dollars and looking in the mirror, tears streaming down my face, full of shame. Every bad choice I'd made had led to that moment. I had no idea what the future held.

I stood in that bathroom for a long time—long enough for one of Stella's kids to knock on the door. I wiped my face, fixed my hair, and walked out into homelessness. We headed for the Atlantic City beach, lugging our few possessions behind us.

That night we found beds in a local shelter. However, when I woke up the following morning, all of my possessions had been stolen. We headed for the beach and set up our makeshift home within sight of the Ferris wheel, the lights of which provided some comfort. The next morning, I took the picture that appears on the cover of this book.

Ironically, the first night wasn't that bad. Actually, it was kind of fun. There was a music festival, and people laughed and danced as the ocean breeze carried the sound of live music. I didn't feel alone with so many other people on the beach, and I tricked myself into thinking of it as an adventure. People shared joints and bottles, and the night passed without incident.

When the first rays of the sun appeared over the Ferris wheel the following morning, I felt a sense of pride. I had survived my first night outside. Maybe things weren't so terrible after all. I would figure it out. Not knowing what lay ahead, I felt slightly invincible, as if I could survive anything.

The second night, however, was one of the worst of my life. Without all the people around, it was eerily quiet. Other than the dim lights from the boardwalk and the flickering ones of the Ferris wheel, it was pitch black. I would come to know those lights, and which bulbs were out, very well over the following two months.

The darkness of that night terrified me, and I didn't sleep a wink. I spent the night huddled beneath our blanket, waiting for the boogeyman to come out and grab me. Rick, per usual, was oblivious and snored next to me. I would rather have been any-where else than on that beach.

The one thing that soothed me was the sound of the waves. Rhythmically, like clockwork, they pounded the shore again and again, reminding me that time was passing and that morning would come. The sun would shine, the seagulls would screech as they searched for food, and people would return to the beach for the day.

I finally felt safe enough to close my eyes. Soon enough, the early morning rays of sunshine rising from the horizon of the Atlantic Ocean flickered across my face. Then, I felt the seagulls walking on our blanket, searching for scraps. I sat up, looked around, and saw the beach had begun to fill with people—early-morning surfers, couples walking hand in hand for a sunrise stroll, and children running in and out of the waves.

And that's when it hit me. Jealousy. It was the first time I experienced it as a homeless person—a feeling that would follow me for many years. I was jealous of something I'd taken for granted my entire life up until that point—normalcy. I'd never realized how wonderful normal could be until that second morning on the beach—dirty, exhausted, and as far removed from normal as a person could be—watching everyone else enjoy their everyday lives.

Sometimes, I think back to that day. Knowing what I know now about the struggles that were to come, I realize how naive I was. If I had known what was coming—the loneliness, the danger, the shame—I would have begged my mother-in-law for a second, and even third, chance.

But, alas, I didn't.

The next two more months passed without significant incidents. The weather was still warm, so there were people around to beg from. We ate lunch every day at Sister Jean's, a local soup kitchen, where we met a man named Junior. He had an apartment nearby and invited us to stay with him one night when a storm was coming. We jumped at the chance to sleep in a warm place and have a shower.

The next morning, Junior offered us a deal. We could stay with him every night as long as we left in the morning and didn't sit in the house all day. I was elated and offered to do all the cooking and cleaning in exchange.

At some point that fall, Rick and I crossed a line. Our relationship became sexual, and as soon as that happened, he became jealous. One night, Rick got drunk and falsely accused Junior of coming on to me. A fight ensued. Another knock on the door.

That time it was the police. They had come to remove Rick from Junior's apartment. I could stay, but Rick was out.

I opted to leave with Rick—another mistake in a long line of bad choices. We left with the officers and explained our situation. They asked if we had anywhere to go, and Rick said we needed to get to New York City.

My last night in Atlantic City ended—my last night of residing in the same state where my children lived. As I gathered our stuff, exhausted, half asleep, and feeling absolutely worthless, I wondered how I'd made so many bad choices in such a short time. There were no excuses, and the shame I felt packing my few meager possessions was palpable. My whole life contained in two bags, not a penny to my name, and no one in my corner.

I felt so sorry for myself that I couldn't think about anything else. I didn't think of my children, my parents, or anyone. All I did was wallow in self-pity and despair. Again, just like the morning at Stella's, I went into the bathroom and looked at myself in the mirror. What a sorry excuse for a woman I'd become. I wanted to lock the door of that bathroom and never come out, but the police were waiting.

As we were escorted out of the building, I looked at the floor as the tears streamed down my face. That humiliation carried over to the bus station, as the officers asked the driver to give us a ride to New York City.

It was one of the lowest moments of my life, and I don't know how I was able to hold it together and get on that bus. As I walked down the aisle to the back row, I was a broken and defeated woman. Once I got to my seat and settled in, I calmed down a bit. It was freezing, and at least I was out of the cold, in a comfortable bus seat, where, for the next three hours, I would be safe.

That calmness lasted until the bus pulled out of the station. As we merged onto the Atlantic City Expressway, the realization of what was happening hit me. I was leaving New Jersey. Leaving my children, and no one even knew it. Not a single soul, other than Rick and the two officers, knew I was headed to New York.

The fact that I was leaving my children ripped a hole in my chest, a hole that is still a gaping wound from which I have not recovered and fear I never will. The further we got from Atlantic City, the more I realized that there was no coming back from that bad decision. I didn't know if or when I would ever see my children again.

CHAPTER 5

Bus Rides

"You will face many defeats in life.
But never let yourself be defeated."
—**Maya Angelou**

Maggie

I'd never before been on a bus, or any form of transportation, where I had no idea what awaited me at the other end. I was literally on the bus to nowhere. Yes, the destination was New York. However, once we arrived, there was no plan, no landing place. Just asphalt, motion, and uncertainty.

Sleep evaded me. I pressed my forehead against the window, watching the blur of barren winter landscape. Rick, of course, slept peacefully, his face slack with the luxury of detachment. My heart pounded louder as we drove through the tunnel into New York. My mouth went dry. I was starving and thirsty, and with no money in my pocket, I had no idea how I was going to eat or drink. As a homeless "noobie," I didn't know we could get water from Starbucks, or go to a drop-in center for food. I didn't know the system, the streets, or even my own limits.

As we stepped off the bus at Port Authority, fear greeted me. People rushed past in a blur of coats and shopping bags, but my attention was drawn to a different of kind of traveler—those who, like me, weren't going anywhere. The homeless population, of which I was now a member.

Their carts and torn shopping bags were filled with everything they still owned, as well as, remnants of lives once lived. These were my people now.

I headed to the nearest bathroom and collapsed into a stall. My stomach was empty, but the nausea surged anyway. I stood there, hunched over the toilet, with the realization that homelessness was now my life. Was it temporary or permanent? I had no idea.

How I had the strength to leave that bathroom is a question I still cannot answer. But just like at Stella's and Junior's, I wiped my face, straightened my coat, and walked out into the abyss that would soon envelop me.

Other than being alone and hungry for the first time in my life, the first few weeks of my life on the streets were uneventful. However, every detail of one morning in December is still fresh in my mind.

The first thing I noticed was the quiet. I'd become used to the continuous hum of the city that never sleeps, so it was the silence that startled me before I'd even opened my eyes. Next was the cold. I was absolutely frozen. Through my blanket, I saw an odd opaqueness and realized it had snowed during the night.

The realization of the task that lay ahead came into focus as I roused myself from sleep and felt the heavy, snow-covered blanket on top of me. Everything I owned was covered in whiteness and had to be moved to a safe location. Where that location was, I had no idea.

That was my first eye-opening experience as a homeless woman in winter on the streets of New York City. I prodded Rick, and with one final sigh, emerged from the blanket. Four or five inches of snow had already accumulated and it was still coming down at a rapid rate. I was not dressed for a snowstorm, and by the time we gathered our things together, I felt the coldest I'd ever been in my life. As I strapped on my backpack and trudged through the streets, snow crept into my shoes, numbing my toes. I wondered again how things had gone so wrong.

Everything I owned now fit into one backpack. It didn't bother me. None of my homeless friends had many belongings, either. That's a funny thing about homelessness—it strips you down. What you don't lose, is stolen. Everything that seems important to you at first becomes less so when you have to carry those things everywhere you go. With a battered self-esteem, I didn't feel entitled to anything, anyway.

Nevertheless, the wish to have some of those things never faded. My high school yearbook, a picture of two of my best friends who had died—Nigel, who was murdered, and Shawn, who committed suicide. They left this world before Facebook, before the term "digital footprint" existed. I'd do anything to see their faces again. Sometimes I would close my eyes and strain to picture their faces, desperate not to forget the curve of Nigel's grin or the way Shawn tilted his head when he laughed.

Rick and I headed over to Park Avenue in the hope of finding a building with an overhang. We were lucky that morning—we found a good spot just off the corner of Park and 30th by the recessed doorway of an office building. I set up what would become our abode for the next two and a half years, carefully unpacking our few possessions and arranging them in our makeshift home. I tried to make it feel like something more than just survival.

Rick went to work immediately. He was a line walker—someone who goes from car to car stopped at a red light, asking for money. I grabbed my *homeless please help me* sign and sat down on the corner, forgoing my coat despite the temperature. I knew what pity looked like. I knew what it took to earn it and make money. Otherwise, Rick would beat me. I'd already learned that lesson and didn't dare sit around and watch him work.

That was four years ago. Before I'd met Traci. Before I'd returned to college. Before I'd crawled—on my hands and knees— off the street.

Maggie panhandling

◆◆◆

Tyson's sudden leap onto my lap broke my nostalgia and snapped me back to the present moment. Georgia started barking, jealous that Tyson was getting my attention. I closed my laptop and went into the kitchen to prepare dinner. I'd have to figure out an excuse about school. And soon. Traci was relentless when she sensed something was off—part detective, part guardian angel. She always knew when I was lying. As much as I admired her skill, I did not like that level of exposure.

Ironically, one of the few benefits of being homeless is how invisible you become. Even as people step over you, you vanish. Despite being an omnipresent sight, it is only a matter of days before no one notices you.

But Traci had noticed me. She'd seen me. And she never stopped watching.

CHAPTER 6

Sandwiches

"If you can't run then walk. If you can't walk then crawl."
—Martin Luther King, Jr.

Traci

Somehow, I knew. It was more because of what Maggie didn't say rather than what she did. For example, she stopped talking about Kristen. The absence became its own kind of presence.

Despite Maggie's silence, I held out hope that Kristen might have convinced Jen to seek treatment because after the day Kristen and I found her slumped on the corner outside the deli, I never saw Jen again.

Next, Maggie stopped asking me to look at her homework assignments, something she'd once done with a kind of pride. The nagging in my stomach grew worse when the semester ended without a glimpse of her report card. I decided not to confront her, however. I waited, knowing that sooner or later, she'd ask me to pay her next tuition bill.

Per usual, Maggie put off the day of reckoning as long as possible. She told me about papers she never submitted and grades she never earned. The deadline for enrolling in summer session passed without further mention of school. In August, I put Maggie out of her misery before she missed the fall semester registration deadline.

"Maggie, I know you dropped your in-person class months ago. Just send me your transcript, and I will get you approved for the fall semester. But you are on your last chance with scholarship money, so don't take more classes than you can handle. There is no rush to graduate. Take one class a semester if you want."

"I'm trying to graduate as quickly as possible," Maggie replied.

I smiled softly, though Maggie's comment cracked something in me. "School, life, and love are marathons, not sprints," I said.

Despite letting Maggie off the hook, guilt crept in. Maybe I'd pushed her too hard. Maybe I'd asked too much of someone still stitching herself back together? It had only been two years since I'd found her sweeping the city sidewalk as if it were the floor of her childhood home. How far and how fast could I expect her to run?

◆ ◆ ◆

The pandemic dragged on along with the winter weather. Days blurred together. Nights unraveled into anxious loops, and I began having difficulty sleeping. Thoughts of the homeless plight in general, and of two women in particular—Jen and Maggie, whose names I did not yet know—kept me up at night. An undefined unease niggled at me along with a strange ache behind my ribs.

For the first time in decades, I dreamt about my mother. Absent from my life while she was alive, she now became a frequent visitor during my sleep, whispering things to me I didn't want to remember. Her ghostly return opened old wounds, unnerving me even more than the sound of omnipresent ambulance sirens.

On many mornings, I awoke more bedraggled than when I'd gone to bed. Joel suggested we cut back on the miles we were walking, but I knew my deteriorating mental and physical condition had nothing to do with miles, muscles, or even the pandemic. Long-suppressed memories and glossed-over wounds were reappearing. My mother's face, once a shadowy image in the far corners of my mind, came back into focus.

Meanwhile, the death toll climbed and the sirens continued. The news that deaths in New York had surpassed 1,000, that thousands of other victims lay in hospitals fighting for their lives, and that the total number of cases in the city had exceeded 60,000 unnerved even the most stoic among us. Added to those fears was the fact that the virus chose its victims randomly. And though Joel and I tried not to say it aloud, we knew we were in the demographic the virus liked best. Still, we walked, refusing to be paralyzed by fear.

Unlike the homeless, however, we had plenty of food. One day, we saw a homeless man eat a dirty slice of leftover pizza he'd found digging through a garbage can, his disgust giving way to his hunger. Before my brain could process what my eyes were witnessing, Joel declared, "Tomorrow we make sandwiches."

The next morning, our kitchen became a battlefield of compassion. Slices of bread on one counter, the peanut butter and jelly on the other. Every morning, even before the birds started chirping, we made sandwiches. Dozens of them. Day after day, Joel and I walked the city streets handing them out until our knees buckled and our feet screamed. In the afternoons, I would go to my private law office, and Joel, a mental health counselor, would speak to his clients on Zoom.

During this period, I first saw Maggie. She wasn't popping the prescription opioids her dentist had prescribed following her emergency root canal, or even chugging her carefully hidden bottle of vodka. Rather, she was doing the most menial of household chores—sweeping. She wasn't cleaning her kitchen floor or garage or back porch. It was the sidewalk, and it wasn't even *her* sidewalk; that particular sidewalk, which she was so carefully sweeping, belonged to New York City.

Covered in grime, tightly gripping the handle of a broken broom, Maggie was intent on sweeping the area around her makeshift home, as if this one vestige of domesticity might keep her from falling into the abyss that already had become her reality. Her oversized gray coat, filled with holes, and her dirty stocking cap barely kept her from shivering in the frigid spring air, despite her brisk movements.

My heart registered what my eyes refused to accept—Maggie, vivacious, proud, and defiant, was homeless. I thought she was mentally ill. I was somewhat afraid of her, which surprised me, not only because Maggie is a woman, but also because she was tiny. I guessed she was about five feet tall and weighed less than one hundred pounds at the time.

Returning to my apartment, I vowed to look for her the following day. When I awoke, I thought of every excuse not to walk downtown. I finally got out of bed, dressed, and, forgoing breakfast, headed in the direction of 30th Street and Park Avenue. A block away, I spotted her. Sweeping. Again.

I reached into the back pocket of my jeans for a few dollars and hesitated, torn between the opposing desires of offering her some money and not wanting to insult her. In the end, the first desire, dictated by my heart, overruled the second centered in my brain. As she accepted the offering from my outstretched hand, our eyes met. I could see her inner light flickering, defying her broken appearance, before she turned and, without acknowledging me, walked away.

I watched Maggie slip beneath a mound of dirty blankets, carefully tucking the few dollars up her sleeve. A sort of "out-of-body" moment enveloped me as I realized that Maggie was the only other human being—woman or man—in view at that moment. Stunned by the silence, I stood there realizing that Maggie and I were just two women breathing the same air but living in vastly different worlds.

It was then that I also realized, much like Alice in Wonderland, we'd fallen through the looking glass. The small loophole in the shelter-in-place edict exposed a new reality to us. We'd left behind the safety of sanitized news clips and crossed into a world where justice was absent, dignity was optional, and survival was its own fragile victory. It was dirty, unnerving, and raw. It soiled our hands, our clothes, and even our souls, forcing us to question humanity, truth, ourselves, and the very structure of the world we all shared.

CHAPTER 7

Broken Brooms

"She crashed, rather spectacularly, on the craggy peaks of rock bottom."
—Donna Ashworth

Maggie

Tired from reading school assignments, I closed my laptop and headed to the kitchen to feed Georgia and Tyson. My hands shook from exhaustion, and some kibble clattered onto the floor. The broom—another small, but necessary, gift from Traci—stood waiting in the corner. I reached for it, the motion automatic. As I swept, I noticed my movements hadn't changed much since my days on the street. Deliberate, thorough, slightly frantic. I remembered a day, cold and foreboding, when hundreds of New Yorkers died every day from COVID. But for some of us, the lucky ones like me, COVID wasn't the end of life.

It was the beginning.

◆ ◆ ◆

By the spring of 2020, Rick and I had accumulated a few household items, including a broken broom, which I used every morning to sweep the sidewalk. But that morning—the morning I first saw Traci—I wasn't thinking about cleanliness. I was thinking about food. I was hungry and needed to eat. It had been five days since the city shut down, and we were starving. I'd become accustomed to eating small amounts of food, having lost over a hundred pounds since becoming homeless. Now, at ninety-six pounds, I didn't need much—just a discarded, stale roll from the nearby deli would suffice. A cup of hot coffee would make my morning meal complete.

My stomach grumbled as I forced myself up and out from under the warmth of the dirty blanket, which covered my even dirtier mattress. At least we now had a mattress, and there was no snow on top of me that morning. The overhang shielded us.

For reasons I never understood, the building superintendent had allowed us to live on that corner as long as we were up and out of the way before the employees arrived in the morning. He'd often coaxed me up with a few dollars to buy a cup of hot coffee from the food truck on the corner.

As I rose to my feet, shaky and hollow, I had no way of knowing that my life was about to change. That a new thread was about to be woven into my story.

Dizzy from hunger, I tidied our "home" and began my morning cleanup routine. A survival ritual more than a necessity. Sweeping the sidewalk had become part of my identity, a performance of dignity in a world that had stripped mine away. I looked up and down the street. Empty. The kind of empty that actually made noise. A quiet, a vacuum that hummed.

Even the few people we saw in those early days of the pandemic did not pay much attention to us. We were shadows. Pariahs. But that morning, the streets were completely empty. There were no employees arriving for work, much less a food truck selling rolls and hot coffee. There was only fear on everyone's mind, and, for a change, it wasn't fear of us.

With the city deserted, I could have skipped my morning routine of sweeping the sidewalk, but I didn't. I grabbed my broken broom. I made my way toward the corner, making sure I swept every bit of the sidewalk, as if every crack and crevice mattered.

And then, I felt her. Before I even saw her, I felt her. A presence. Solid. Watching. An older woman staring at me, hand outstretched. She stood very still, her eyes locked on mine. *Why was she staring at me? And why wasn't she in her apartment where she would be safe?* Her presence was both comforting—there was no one else on the street—and unnerving.

I'd lost my glasses years before that day and was legally blind without them. Nevertheless, I willed my eyes to focus. She was holding something. Paper, fluttering in the wind.

As I grew closer, I could tell she was offering me money. However, years on the street had taught me to be careful. I was desperate, so I approached her warily. *Why was she helping me? Why was she not afraid to come near me?* Everyone else seemed to think all homeless people had the virus.

I was too hungry and desperate to give it much consideration that morning. Like a dog slowly approaching a stranger offering a bone, I inched closer and snatched the money from her outstretched hand. Too scared to even say thank you, I turned and walked away. I never felt so rude in my life. I shrugged it off. I thought I would never see her again, anyway.

I was wrong. I did see her again. The very next day, and the day after that, and every day for months. She returned. Steady, consistent, unafraid.

She was an attorney. A woman who had built her life in a world I no longer believed I could access. She noticed me. Not just as a person, but as someone worth seeing. Despite our outward realities, that initial encounter was the beginning of a friendship and a personal transformation that would impact far more than my living conditions.

A radical reorganization of my reality—inside as well as out—had begun.

Swim Races and Clowns

"Nobody is going to pour the truth into your head.
It's something you have to find for yourself."
—**Noam Chomsky**

Traci

In August of 2022, Maggie registered for the fall semester, determined to take two classes. I urged her to take one—and only online—but she insisted she could handle two. She needed an in-person seminar on medieval literature, and that one was only taught in the fall.

September arrived, and school began. There was a hint of momentum in her life, a sort of forward movement that felt unfamiliar but promising. As luck would have it, Kristen was in her seminar class, a gentle reminder that maybe, just maybe, the universe was aligning. We learned the good news that Jen had returned home and was in an in-person treatment center in Florida. The bad news was that when Jen could no longer get a prescription for opioids, she'd turned to heroin.

Maggie and I both understood that heroin addiction was not just a detour, it was a cliff. One of Maggie's best friends—the girl named Melissa—was a heroin addict and had cycled through recovery and relapse several times in the year I'd known her. Like an echo, heroin didn't just destroy lives, it haunted them.

Maggie turned forty-one that month, and we celebrated with manicures, her first in four years. Her hands, rough and weathered, told the story of her life on the street—the omnipresent dirt under her nails that never seemed to go away regardless of the amount of scrubbing and the thickness of the nailbed itself. A person living on the street needs thick nails for protection.

As we sat in side-by-side chairs in the nail salon, our hands outstretched, Maggie wanted to know the story of how a girl from Virginia ended up walking the streets of New York City, handing out sandwiches. Specifically, for the first time, she asked me about my relationship with my mother. Up until that point, most of our conversations had been about Maggie and her mother, her past, her pain. Now, she wanted to know me—not the woman who showed up with sandwiches but the one underneath.

I was determined to steer clear of anything significant, yet that was never an easy task when talking about my childhood. I tried to divert her attention by talking about a safer subject—how I'd first met Joel—a story which included a little bit about my mother, but only slightly grazed the surface of my secret.

◆◆◆

In June 1977, I graduated from Virginia Tech and was preparing for law school at William & Mary in Williamsburg, Virginia. I had a summer job as a restaurant hostess.

One day toward the end of the summer, my mother announced that she'd submitted my resume to a government agency—the Federal Mediation and Conciliation Service—and they wanted to interview me. She was intent on taking me to the interview the following morning. I balked. The summer was almost over. However, true to her nickname, *The Big Chief*, my mother insisted.

The next morning, I found myself in my mother's car on our way to the interview. The agency needed an intern for the last four weeks of summer, and they offered double what I was making at the restaurant. Despite my initial hesitation, I accepted the job on the spot.

Joel had a job at the same agency. His office had an extra desk in it where the summer intern worked. Before the summer was over, we'd become a couple.

I've often thought about how unlikely it was for me to ever have had that job. And the one and only reason was because of my mother. Without her insistence, I would never have applied for the job. Her persistence, that unrelenting force I often resented, set everything in motion.

The following summer, Joel was reassigned to the New York City office, and we were married. I transferred law schools. We packed our few possessions into my mustard-colored Toyota Celica, a twenty-first birthday gift from my grandmother, and headed north. As nice as that little car was, it was literally my only possession. I had less than a thousand dollars in my bank account. But I was young, naïve, and brave.

We settled into our first apartment in Brooklyn Heights, a small residential area just east of the Brooklyn Bridge and directly across from Manhattan. It was conveniently located walking distance from my new law school and a short subway ride to Joel's office. At five hundred dollars a month rent, it felt like a palace. We had the top floor of a single-family, free-standing brownstone, with windows on all sides, as well as access to the roof, providing a fantastic place to sunbathe amidst the spectacular views of the East River.

Joel continued to work, and I finished law school. After graduating in 1980, I landed my first professional job at a large pharmaceutical company, where I worked for the next thirty years. Flush with two salaries and no children, we bought a renovated brownstone in the same neighborhood, ignoring the staggering thirteen percent mortgage rates.

The building housed three apartments. We lived in the duplex on the first and second floors. The monthly rent from the two rental units on the third and fourth floors, paid our mortgage. Young, in love, and money in our pockets, our reality was very far removed from the *World of Warcraft* where Maggie had met her husband.

◆ ◆ ◆

Now, forty years later, I sat in a nail salon with Maggie by my side, reminiscing about how we'd first met in the early days of the pandemic. Even the least afraid among us were unnerved. The constant sirens, refrigerated vans with bodies awaiting burial, and the nightly tributes to the healthcare workers made it impossible to hide from the truth.

Nevertheless, Joel and I set out every morning, trying to carve meaning out of a senseless time, our bags full of sandwiches, water, and granola bars, and our hearts full of hope. At first, we had no specific destination in mind, and, other than our goal of handing out the food, no specific purpose, either. A quiet sense that doing nothing was a worse option than doing something imperfectly propelled us forward. There were days when one of us would try to convince the other to skip our morning routine of sandwich making and delivery, but the other one would insist that we were going out. We clung tightly to each other, unified in a common battle against a common enemy.

On some days that enemy was the virus. On other days, it was our fear. When one of us would suggest quitting, the other would restate the obvious—we didn't really have a good choice. We felt it was impossible to shelter in our apartment, looking out the windows at hungry people.

I knew where Maggie lived, and every day I set out to find her. For several weeks, I walked by her and Rick and offered them a sandwich and a few dollars. We rarely spoke more than a few words—or stayed on their corner more than a minute—until one day Maggie stopped me as we were leaving and asked me a question.

"Do you know why the money is so important to us?"

"To buy food?"

"No, to use the bathroom at McDonald's," Maggie replied.

"You have to pay to use the bathroom?"

"Not exactly. You have to buy something to be able to use it, but even a cup of coffee or tea is enough."

I was shocked—more at the realization that it had never occurred to me to question how or where homeless people used bathrooms than from the news that now there were very few available. In fact, during the early months of the pandemic the only public bathroom in the area was at McDonald's on Park Avenue, two blocks south of Maggie's corner.

Small amounts of money represented not just sustenance, but self-respect. Sleeping on the street, panhandling for money, wearing dirty clothes, all appeared tolerable. However, for the most part, relieving oneself on the street (at least of the more embarrassing form of human waste) was avoided whenever possible.

The pandemic surged on, along with the prolonged winter temperatures and a scarcity of food. The weather matched the mood that spring—dark, foreboding, cold. Even the tulips, one of the first early signs of spring, were reluctant to peek their heads above ground. Somehow, even they seemed to understand that all was not okay in our world.

No one knew what to do to fight the virus other than keeping distance from other people and frequent hand washing. Ironically, at first, New Yorkers were advised not to wear masks. That changed on April 15 when they became mandatory. At the same time, auxiliary hospital beds appeared in the Javits Convention Center, in field tents in Central Park, and in the recently arrived naval hospital ship, the *USNS Comfort*. But not much was done to help the thousands of homeless people starving on the city's empty streets. No one handed them masks, hand sanitizer, or even food. They remained invisible.

The days turned into weeks, which turned into months. Little by little, Maggie and I shared our personal stories. I told her a few insignificant things about my childhood—that I'd grown up in Virginia and had spent my youth as a competitive swimmer, careful to leave out any mention of my mother.

In turn, she told me that she was the daughter of two Jewish school teachers who had retired to Florida. Born into a good family and raised in Brooklyn along with a younger sister she adored, she admitted having been given every opportunity in life.

"So, you had a good childhood?" I asked, somewhat surprised.

"Yeah, I did. My parents were pretty cool, all things considered."

In our first months together, Maggie was under the impression that I'd never faltered and had lived a charmed life. She was surprised to learn, like her, my family had been middle class.

"I thought you were some sort of trust-fund baby," she said.

"No trust funds here, but I was given a good education. My dad paid for college and law school, so I graduated debt-free. That is a blessing that can make a big difference."

"It sure can," Maggie agreed. "I went to college too." I wondered why a college-educated woman would end up homeless but decided not to ask her about it that morning.

A few weeks later, Maggie told me a story of when her mother, furious over Maggie's latest infraction, had cut up her favorite stuffed clown, Mr. George. In response, still not wanting to say anything about my own mother, I told her about the day I'd won two blue ribbons in a swim race.

◆ ◆ ◆

I was six years old and had just won my first two swim races in the eight-and-under age group. Twenty-five meters of freestyle. Twenty-five meters of backstroke. When I pulled my tiny body out of the water after my second first-place finish, the coach ran over and picked me up. My teammates cheered. We won the meet with the points earned from my second victory.

I looked around for my parents. My father was smiling, with his thumb straight up in the air. Even my mother, normally devoid of any visible emotion, sported a slight grin. How I craved her love, or even her passing attention. So acute was my desire that I was willing to do just about anything to get it.

High above my coach's head, the summer breeze tantalizing my wet skin, the misguided message about life entered my consciousness—winners are admired; winners are loved. It would be another sixty years before I learned that, while it is often true winners are admired, admiration has very little, if anything, to do with love. Despite our different approaches to finding it, like Maggie, I'd been chasing love my entire life. And, as with so many of us, I was looking for it outside of myself in the form of accomplishments, recognition, and success.

◆◆◆

That seemingly innocuous story had opened a Pandora's Box. I thought about the irony of it for the remainder of the day. A destroyed stuffed clown and a swimming ribbon. Two talismans of childhood learning.

That night, my mother made her first actual "appearance" in my bedroom. No longer a hazy figure in a dream, she stood by my bed holding those two blue ribbons. I couldn't move. My throat closed. For the first time in my life, I considered the possibility that I might be experiencing a nervous breakdown.

It was also the first moment I realized that my connection to Maggie had something to do with the loss of my mother. My bond with her wasn't just about compassion. It was grief. Grief for my mother. Grief for the girl I'd once been, trying so hard to earn love. I couldn't save my mother, but maybe, just maybe, I could walk with Maggie toward a different ending.

The next morning, I woke up crying. Then I dried my eyes and put on my big-girl pants, determined to forge ahead.

Onward, soldiers!

CHAPTER 9

Chasing Darkness

"If there was no suffering, you would never search for the truth."
—**Osho**

Maggie

By October, things were looking up. I was halfway through the fall semester and doing well. For the first time in what felt like forever, I allowed myself to feel cautiously optimistic. My parents had moved back to New York, and despite my father's deteriorating health, my mother and I had never been closer. Still, I knew the peace I felt was fragile.

In early November, it began to unravel. I realized I'd made a mistake by signing up for two classes again. The pressure had built up quietly, like water rising behind a dam. I dropped my in-person seminar, which was only taught in the fall. *How was it possible that Traci had given me a second chance and I'd already blown it?* At that moment, it didn't matter.

I knew I had to pass that seminar class sooner or later because it was a required course. I also knew that was not going to be easy. And now, because I'd dropped it twice, I'd lose my scholarship from Traci's foundation. But my main concern was not the money. It was Traci. I couldn't bear the thought of her knowing I'd failed again.

Nevertheless, I went straight to the financial assistance department and applied for two New York State college tuition grants. Then I went home and did something unusual for me. I prayed, childlike, almost begging.

I was sick to my stomach at the thought that Traci would find out I'd dropped another class. I knew I should have told her the truth, right then and there. Per usual, however, I didn't. I slipped back into the familiar cycle of avoidance, a self-sabotaging pattern I'd rehearsed all my life. *What was wrong with me?* I was furious with myself. I could not believe I'd done it again, even knowing that I could have told Traci the truth.

I had no excuse. Traci had proven herself to be supportive over and over in the two and a half years we'd known each other. No matter what I did—or didn't do—she was always there, like a lighthouse on the hill with its omnipresent glow. In fact, it was Traci's friendship that had given me the confidence to finally leave Rick. Compared to that decision, dropping a class here or there was insignificant. But shame isn't logical. It burrows into your bones and tells you that you're always failing, even when you're doing your best.

◆ ◆ ◆

By the summer of 2020, Traci had become more than just a kind stranger. Our growing friendship helped me regain some of my lost confidence. I found myself looking forward to her visits more than I liked to admit.

Nevertheless, every time I saw her, I was convinced it would be the last. Homeless people know this syndrome. Sometimes a person would show up every day for several weeks with a few dollars or some food, but eventually they would disappear.

But Traci and Joel didn't disappear. Rain or shine, they brought food, conversation, dignity. That was enough to get us through the day. I let down my guard and began to count on her daily visits and the budding friendship we enjoyed.

For the most part, I told Traci the truth about what had led to my homelessness. She never judged me, and when I revealed the story about my addiction to opioids, she shrugged and said her mother had been a Valium addict. Nevertheless, I also told her some lies. I wanted her to be my friend. She was a lawyer. I was a homeless woman. How could she be interested in me? The first lie I told her was when I'd said I was a college graduate, the words tumbling out of my mouth like a reflex. I told myself it was harmless, but I knew better. I was certain Traci would find out and dump me. The worst part is that she had not even asked. I just volunteered the lie.

I remember exactly when my proclivity for telling fibs started. One day, my mother was yelling at me for something I wanted to do—I don't remember exactly what it was—and my dad came into my bedroom and said to tell my mother whatever she wanted to hear, and then to do whatever I wanted. That advice stuck. It became a blueprint for survival,

Another thing that shaped my life was the way my mother responded when I didn't live up to her expectations. To this day, despite our greatly improved relationship, the fear of disappointing her lives inside me. She was, and still is, a handful. She is fragile and fierce, quick with criticism, slow with praise. She wields her words as weapons. She is set in her ways and does not quite understand the meaning of "unconditional" mother's love. However, I am not throwing stones. I've lost custody of my own children.

Sadly, given my history, I was not that surprised when I lied to Traci. I know why I did it—the same reason I told everyone I met on the street that I was a college graduate. I wanted to be taken seriously. I wanted people to know that I was not like the other homeless people. It was important to me that people knew that I was smart, that I once had a life, and that I was still worth something.

If I had been able to graduate from college, people would know I was intelligent. Thus, I was less likely to be feared, and possibly more likely to be helped. I didn't think much of the lie at the time; it was important Traci knew I was not just another drug abuser on the sidewalk.

I'd had a chance to make a change with Traci, and I blew it. Every time I met someone new, I had a choice. I could begin the new relationship with honesty and keep it that way, or, true to form, I could lie to the person for whatever reason seemed important at the time. I didn't even have to say anything. Traci didn't ask me about my educational background. But of course, I couldn't help myself. Once I'd told her that first lie, I felt I'd already ruined everything. The second lie came easier. The following week, I told her I had a graduate degree in psychology.

Despite lying about my educational background, there were certain things I would never lie about when I was on the street— things I considered absolutely off the table, no matter what. That included referring to children, pretending to be pregnant, or saying a family member was sick. I felt that it was bad karma and would often get angry when I heard other homeless people using those tricks on pedestrians.

As my bond with Traci deepened, I began to suspect that she knew when I was lying. There were small comments here and there, or questions she would ask, that made me realize I wasn't fooling her. This realization was shocking, because I thought I was a pretty good liar. The fact that Traci had seen through my lies was also alarming.

In case you're wondering why I never graduated from college, I'd like to make up some story about an illness, injury or unexpected death in my family. But it wasn't any of those things. The truth was much harder to admit. It was because of a guy. His name was Danny, and I thought he was the most beautiful man I'd ever seen. He was also utterly destructive, and the reason my mother ripped apart my prized stuffed clown, Mr. George.

Ours was no ordinary love affair. It was a ten-year obsession that led not only to Mr. George's destruction, but to my own and countless others, as well. Regardless, like so many love-obsessed women, I clung to it until there was nothing left. I thought Danny was the light I'd been chasing all my life.

I was wrong. He was the darkness.

That darkness led me to the streets of New York City. And if that was not in and of itself a difficult life, we were now in the middle of a global pandemic with nothing other than concrete under my feet. But Traci was there with me, and her friendship and steadfast acceptance of my shortcomings gave me the courage to do something I'd been putting off for a long time.

Despite the chilly temperature that May morning, I woke up in a cold sweat. I somehow knew that the task ahead would irrevocably destroy my relationship with Rick, who'd been my only safety on the streets for the previous three years. However, doing nothing would mean surrendering the last pieces of myself. Despite my fear, I was determined. I felt the sun on my face—a good start—and gathered my strength.

I tried to remember what a spring morning in New York City smelled like before I'd lost my sense of taste and smell. Morning dew on the trees that grew on Park Avenue. The aroma of fresh coffee and bacon wafting over from the food cart parked on the corner across the street.

A garbage truck's beeping, unforgiving in the morning's silence, interrupted my thoughts. *Why were they even out here now? There was no trash to collect, anyway.* I found the courage to open my eyes and let the city sharpen into focus. It was early. I could tell the time by the color of the sky and the shadows.

My suspicions were confirmed when I saw the seagulls overhead—a pair, they always came to search for scraps. Today, they found none. Hunger didn't leave any scraps behind.

Absentmindedly, I touched the side of my face. A familiar feeling awaited me. Another bruise. Another black eye. Another day of explanations. I was sure Traci would notice. As I got up from my mattress, my whole body ached, and I felt much older than my thirty-eight years.

The last and final thing I noticed was the taste in my mouth. Ironic, since I'd not tasted anything in three years, since the day I'd fallen backward onto the sidewalk and injured my head. But my tongue still responded to stimuli, and that morning, what I could "taste" was an overwhelming sense of salt and brine. I knew what it was. Blood. My own.

As I got up from my makeshift bed, exhausted, sore and defeated, the remembered taste of blood in my mouth, I steadied myself to take the next step that would forever change my life. No more beatings. No more mornings waking up on the sidewalk, my body and spirit conquered. Last night would be the last. I needed a few days to put my plan into action. But the decision was made.

Adrenalin flooded my system, squelching my fear.

And I began to move.

CHAPTER 10

An Elusive Truth

"Awareness of ignorance is the beginning of wisdom."
—**Socrates**

Traci

It became apparent that Maggie lied to me more often than I wanted to believe. While it was difficult, I finally learned to accept Maggie's untruthfulness as her "area of opportunity," as we said in Corporate America, or her "bugaboo," as we said in Virginia. I view people's strengths and weaknesses like pick-up sticks. We all have the same number and color in the box, but each time they are thrown down, they create a different arrangement. Some arrangements are easy to pick up, and some are more challenging. And even though I rarely lie, I have plenty of my own shortcomings to worry about.

Ironically, Maggie's tendency to fib reminded me of my friend Joyce's chronic lateness. Regardless of the importance of the appointment, she just couldn't be on time. I realized Joyce was not going to change, so if I wanted to remain in a relationship with her, I was the one who had to adjust. I compensated. If she said she'd meet me at noon, I'd show up at 12:20.

I made the same type of adjustment with Maggie and eventually realized that whatever she said might—or might not—be true. I changed my expectations. I stopped assuming what Maggie said was true unless she offered some sort of proof. She intuitively figured this out and started to offer evidence. For example, she always sent me a picture when she was on campus, so I'd know she'd made it. I also learned that if Maggie did not offer such corroboration, chances were whatever she said was not true.

Maggie at school

And then, almost by magic, something changed between us. The more Maggie trusted me, the more truthful she became. There were instances when she thought I would really give it to her for lying about this or that, but when she finally told me the truth, I'd already figured it out and didn't react.

Nevertheless, when you lose your trust in someone, there is often a slow, yet discernable, deterioration in the relationship. Trust, once lost, is difficult to regain. Hence, as with my friend Joyce, there were many days when I struggled to remain in a relationship with Maggie. Yet, I was determined to do so.

That choice caused a slight shift in my consciousness. In accepting Maggie for who she was, I became less judgmental of others and far more accepting of their shortcomings. Ironically, in doing so, I began to afford myself the same favorable treatment. Years of self-denial, self-recrimination, and otherwise negative thoughts began to dissipate.

I started to love and approve of myself. Gone was my lifelong incessant need for achievement. I no longer had any self-created mountains to climb, races to win, degrees to earn. The pressure to prove my self-worth lifted. There was nothing left for me to do but to just be present.

This was the first of many gifts my relationship with Maggie gave me. The second was the return, and eventual forgiveness, of my mother.

My mother continued to *appear*. Most of the time, she was just sort of *there* in my mind. On occasion, she'd make her presence felt in ways that brushed up against the physical world. For example, once I could not find my keys after searching in all the usual places. I *heard* her tell me to look inside her jewelry box, the one relic of hers I kept on my bedroom dresser. I'd never once put my keys inside that old box. But there they were. On other occasions, I *heard* her repeat the words, "Resist nothing," which meant absolutely nothing to me at the time.

My mother's constant presence brought back memories of my youth. For example, as far back as I can remember, I never wanted to be dependent on anyone—not my mother, not a man. Even as a young girl, I knew I wanted to work, to earn money, to be able to take care of myself. I got my first job the summer I turned thirteen, handing out scorecards, balls, and putters at the putt-putt golf course at our town pool. I earned a dollar an hour and worked five hours a day, five days a week. That was twenty-five dollars a paycheck—good money for a young girl growing up in Virginia fifty years ago.

At sixteen, I had my first date. We went to the high school football game on a Friday night, and afterward, to the local diner. When the check arrived, I opened my purse and put a ten-dollar bill on the table to cover the cost of my hamburger and soda. My date was so taken aback he couldn't speak. Societal norms in Virginia dictated that the boy pay for a date.

The summer before my senior year in high school, I decided I was going to be a lawyer. I remember the exact moment. I was shopping. I still had a year of high school and four years of college in front of me. But the plan was set.

I'm not sure where the desire came from, but if I had to guess—and I'm being serious—it was probably from watching *Perry Mason*. The search for justice inspired me.

Interestingly, when I announced my intention to become a lawyer, not a single person in my family said I couldn't—or shouldn't—do it. That kind of support was something I took for granted as a young girl. Now, I realize it was a blessing. Despite growing up in Virginia in a traditional family setting, I never felt less than the boys. Perhaps the fact that my mother attended

George Washington University on a basketball scholarship had more of an influence on me than I understood at the time.

Unlike Maggie's experience, my mother never told me that I was unworthy, not good enough, or otherwise deficient. Despite the pain of her death, and the ensuing feelings that she had abandoned me, oddly, my self-worth and confidence remained intact.

Nevertheless, I'd spent an entire lifetime lying to myself. Telling myself that my mother was not important to me. That I never loved her. All in the misguided belief that those lies would separate me from the pain—and embarrassment—of her untimely death. But all that accomplished was to separate me from her love and create a gap between us and within myself.

That internal gap widened. An imaginary demon started chasing me, and it soon became clear it was not going to stop. And so, I started running away from it, down the deserted streets of New York City, and into the arms of a homeless woman who would forever change my life.

Every morning, Joel would ask where I wanted to walk. Eventually, he stopped asking. He knew we were going down Park Avenue to the outdoor farmers' market at Union Square. Oddly, I would not think of walking that far now. But those were unusual days, and our world had shrunk to blocks and hours. Time was suspended.

Like fighting a war, there was not much to do other than to survive another day. A long walk chewed up a lot of time, and handing out sandwiches kept our minds off our own suffering. Life had all but come to a standstill, and no one knew when the pandemic would end.

That's when I first noticed it or was conscious of noticing it. Something extraordinary happened. Despite the unrest about my mother and the pandemic, I felt happy. In fact, I was the happiest I'd ever been in my life. *How could this possibly be?* The other strange thing I noticed was that when I woke up in the morning, I was calm, even if some mornings, exhausted. This was a sharp contrast to my pre-pandemic life when I'd often wake up seized by terror. Over nothing. It was just an overall feeling of fear. It lasted ten years, and then, without explanation, faded away during the pandemic

While Joel knew where we were going, he did not yet know why. Perhaps, I did not consciously know it, either. I now know I was looking for Maggie. One morning as we passed her corner, we spotted Rick. Maggie was not there. I didn't think much about it at the time and continued downtown with the intention of handing out our sandwiches. On the way back, I spotted her running down Park Avenue.

"Can we talk?" she asked.

"What's up?"

Maggie hesitated, and then made the rather vague claim, "Rick is a great guy, even though sometimes he gets a little handsy."

"You mean he hits you?"

"Not exactly. He pushes me around," she admitted.

"No one can abuse you unless you allow it."

"Rick is family, and I feel obligated to protect him."

"Protecting him is fine; allowing him to abuse you is something else. How long has this been going on?"

Maggie's head dropped, and a tear rolled down her left cheek. "Very soon after our arrival in New York, Rick stopped being nice to me. He said I couldn't sit and watch him work all day. He made a cardboard sign and sat me on the corner and told me not to get up until I'd made at least twenty dollars. I was so embarrassed. I kept my head down the entire time and refused to speak to anyone."

"You didn't make any money, right?"

"Nope. When Rick came back a few hours later and saw my empty cup, he slapped me across the face. He told me I had to get over my shame and ask every single person that walked by for help. If they didn't help, we didn't eat, and, more importantly, we didn't smoke."

"So, you started panhandling?"

"Yes. I made my own sign and sat down. I must have looked so ashamed because a man stopped and gave me two dollars and a cigarette. He introduced himself and said he worked around the corner. He promised to come back later and check on me, and I burst into tears. I couldn't believe someone was kind enough to help me. That gave me a boost in confidence, and I raised my head."

"Then what happened?"

"It's a funny story. I found a *New York Times* and started to do the crossword puzzle to take my mind off things. A man stopped and asked me if I had gotten eighteen across. When I told him the answer, he handed me ten dollars. When Rick came back to check on me, I'd made twenty-seven dollars. I was proud of myself. I wasn't going to get slapped again. Or so I thought."

"That was over two years ago, right?"

"Yeah."

Maggie lowered her head and cried for a second time, but it was not just a single tear rolling down her cheek. It was an all-out sobbing that seemed to arise from her heart, rather than her eyes. I froze, dumbstruck, unable to find words to express the conflicting emotions I felt.

I knew Rick would not wake up one morning and realize that he shouldn't do it. Abuse doesn't work that way. Addiction had stolen whatever goodness remained. And even if that realization emerged, he would not have been able to stop. His outbursts were activated by drugs and alcohol. Only Maggie could save herself.

I didn't know what to do. I didn't dare hug Maggie—COVID was everywhere—so I settled for a lame piece of advice. "No one can stop abuse except the abused person."

The next morning, Maggie was waiting for me. Per usual, she was sitting on her folding chair, reading the newspaper. "We need to talk," she said. "Rick beat me up *real* bad this morning. I ran down Park Avenue screaming for help. This was the second time in the past two days."

My stomach cramped as I looked over at Rick. He seemed fragile and vulnerable, yet, like Maggie once did, I was learning more about his dark side.

I went home with two things on my mind. The first was a strong desire that Maggie would do something to protect herself from Rick's temper. The second was concern over the upcoming subway shutdown, allegedly to clean the cars to ensure the elimination of possible COVID germs.

The planned overnight shutdown was the first complete closure since the subway system had opened a hundred years earlier. At that point, we knew several people who slept in the subway tunnels to escape the nighttime temperatures, and despite donating the spare blankets and quilts in our apartment, they were cold.

The next morning, I saw Maggie running toward me, arms in the air, shouting loudly. I wasn't sure if she was laughing or crying. With Maggie, both things could happen simultaneously. I approached her with caution.

And held my breath.

CHAPTER 11

Spring Escapes

"You are never destroyed by anyone except yourself."
—Viktor Frankl

Maggie

At 9:00 a.m., I told Rick I was headed to the bathroom at McDonald's. My voice was calm, so ordinary it betrayed nothing. But the truth was I had no intention of going inside. Not yet. My heart pounded, my palms damp with sweat. I crossed the street with purpose, eyes fixed on the public phone like it was a lifeline. I didn't stop to use the bathroom. I just went straight to that phone, picked up the receiver, and dialed Lina's number from memory, each digit like a heartbeat. One ring. Two. Three.

After three rings, Lina answered. "Hello?" I heard the fear in her voice even before she said, "Who is this?" It was rare for anyone to call her work phone so early. I took a deep breath. That was all I had to say.

She knew. She had been waiting months to hear those words. I had been circling this moment gathering courage, and now I had taken the leap. I was breathless when I hung up. For the first time in years, I felt weightless. Elated. Alive.

I hung up the phone. I thought I was finally free and couldn't wait to tell Traci. I knew she would be so proud of me. How I craved her approval. I could barely contain myself. I sat on my folding chair waiting for her, buzzing with the kind of energy that makes you feel invincible. And then, there she was, walking down Park Avenue like she always did, with her calm and steady presence.

"I did it! I did it"

Traci blinked. "Did what?"

"I called my caseworker."

"And?"

"She got me into a safe haven room. I'll be living in the Travelers, on Eighth Avenue!"

"How did she find a room so quickly? I thought that took months."

I looked her in the eyes and said it out loud, the thing I had been hiding behind makeup and silence: "Because Rick was beating me again. Women in danger get priority."

Traci's smile wavered. "Wow. Well, bad reason, great result. How long do you have the room?"

"Indefinitely!" I shouted, unable to contain the joy. I started jumping up and down like a kid on a trampoline, wild with relief. People stared. Traci stared. But I didn't care. I thought I was free. Really free.

But freedom, as I soon learned, can be just another illusion.

And then, true to form, life threw me another curve ball. Or maybe, just maybe, I threw it at myself in an unconscious effort to wake up.

That night, in my safe haven room, everything felt surreal. A hot shower. A bed with clean sheets. Four walls that didn't threaten to collapse on me. For the first time in ages, I slept without one eye open. For that night, I believed in peace. But the peace didn't last. The rules started pressing in. I had to check in every three days. I had to show up. I had to be accountable. And before long, I started to feel like a prisoner in the very place that was supposed to save me.

Rick was jealous and thought I was having an affair. He lurked on every corner, always waiting. Every morning, he'd ask me who I'd slept with the night before. Always accusing, never believing. That was a joke. I'd never once cheated on him. But to be fair, it wasn't just Rick's jealousy that made me resent showing up at the Travelers.

Everyone who knows I was homeless says the same thing: *I could never do that. I would never be able to survive those kinds of conditions or that life.* I suppose I thought the same thing when I first found myself on the sidewalk. However, I did survive, and I not only survived, but sort of thrived. I made friends. I found food. I made money. I learned how to be homeless. It's hard to describe the freedom of being homeless. Other than the need to find food, there are no responsibilities.

There is a kind of peace in being homeless. I would not have been able to explain it to anyone before, but now I can. In addition, as crazy as it sounds, I missed the danger. The filth. The chaos. Because for all its brutality, life on the street had given me something I hadn't had in years: freedom. No bills. No appointments. No expectations. Just the wind, the pavement, the centering-energy of truth, of now.

On the street, all that existed was the present moment. And in that moment, I was alive. There was no future to strive toward, no goals to achieve, no mountains to climb. We just lived, moment to moment, as if each moment were our last. And for many of us, it was.

Once I was no longer homeless, that peace was gone. It had been replaced with a certain level of reprieve—I was no longer hungry, or cold, or afraid. But I was no longer at peace, either.

In the safe haven room peace turned into pressure. Pressure to clean myself up, to check in, to act like someone who had their life together. I tried. God knows I tried. I've always adapted—beach, sidewalk, subway station, wherever. But this room? I couldn't make it fit. I couldn't breathe in there.

There was another issue with my safe haven room. I never slept that well on the streets, but I couldn't sleep well there, either. It was too quiet, too still, too stifling. I couldn't stay inside for long periods unless I was sleeping. As soon as I woke up, I had to be back outside. After three years on the street, the streets were my home. I felt trapped in that room. The streets, as scary, filthy, and cold as they were, equaled freedom.

My resentment at having to show up once every three days to sign in, coupled with my general discomfort at being inside, led to the loss of my room. I started feeling like my safe haven room was a prison. It wasn't long before they took it away. I was terrified Traci would find out. Once again, I became dirty. My clothes started to smell. My hair became oily. It was only a matter of time before Traci would notice. I started making up excuses so I'd be ready when she finally said something.

I've realized something lately. Despite the danger, dirt, and hunger, I think I actually liked being homeless because, in addition to the freedom, I was the star of the homeless community. I was the smartest, the most educated, the most together. In essence, I was the number one homeless person in the city, and everyone knew it and respected me for this. We all live in our own little bubbles of reality, as Traci likes to say. And the homeless community is no different. That realization reminded me of when I was in high school.

◆ ◆ ◆

I was one of the smartest kids in my elementary and middle schools. This ensured my acceptance at Kingsborough, an elite high school for the smartest students. For the first time since I'd started kindergarten, I was surrounded by kids who were just like me—top students who excelled at academics.

The classes were challenging. The campus was beautiful. The library was a dream, the cafeteria better than any I'd seen. Still, I felt invisible. No longer exceptional. Just one of many. I hated it. I craved the spotlight I'd grown used to.

This didn't sit well with me for some reason, and I actively looked for excuses to leave the school. I didn't like the commute, the kids were obnoxious, and the extracurricular activities were too much. I finally complained enough that my parents agreed to pull me out and let me attend my neighborhood high school.

Once at South Shore, I was cream of the crop again. I was in the Scholars Institute with fourteen other "top tier" kids and third in line for valedictorian. I took five AP classes my senior year. But I messed around, cut school, and smoked a bunch of weed. I started throwing parties at my house during school hours, and they were a ton of fun until my parents went to open-school night. I will never forget walking into my math class with my parents, all three of us donning our little name badges. My teacher said, "Oh, so you're Maggie," before turning to my parents and saying, "I've never seen her before." The parties ended that day, and I went back to being a star student in the Scholars Institute.

Leaving Kingsborough set the tone for my life. I know that if I had stayed there, I would have been accepted at my dream school—Syracuse University—and I would have had a good career, a home, and money in the bank. But I didn't. Because I needed to feel special. And by chasing that feeling, I ran straight into Danny. The man who almost destroyed me.

No, as Nietzsche said, no one destroys you—you destroy yourself.

And now, I finally understand what he meant.

CHAPTER 12

Prison Walls

*"Everything can be taken from a man but one thing:
the last of the human freedoms—to choose one's attitude
in any given set of circumstances."*
—**Viktor Frankl**

Traci

The following week, I started to suspect Maggie was sleeping on the streets again. One morning before dawn, I skipped my usual cup of coffee and headed downtown. The streets were still cloaked in shadows, the city holding its breath as the sun rose over the East River. Walking between darkness and light, hope and despair, bracing myself for what I already knew in my heart. As light reclaimed the world, birds flew overhead, their songs a melody demanding my attention. And then I saw her, curled up in Rick's arms, asleep on their dirty mattress.

I stopped in my tracks. The sight of her there, folded into that life again, felt like a blow. Not because I was angry, but because I could not understand why she would rather sleep outside with a man who might beat her when she woke up than in her safe haven room. We'd even decorated it with a new flowered comforter for her bed, a few knick-knacks, some of her favorite books, and all the toiletries she could possibly need. It wasn't perfect, but it was warm. It was hers.

I decided not to ask her about it. I didn't have the courage. Or maybe I knew she could not explain it in a way I would understand. Instead, I tried to figure out what would cause her to choose the danger of the streets over the safety of her room. Despite reflecting on the question for many weeks, I never came up with any meaningful answers. I was still too tethered in my own sense of logic, of order. At that point, my reality was just too different. To me, voluntarily returning to the streets was akin to voluntarily returning to prison.

Observing Maggie's choice to give up her safe haven room caused me to reflect on the broader issue of prison cells. Maggie was not alone in erecting them. There were other New Yorkers who stayed inside, so-called sheltering-in-place, essentially making themselves prisoners in their own homes. I'd seen how fear became a cell.

Joel and I had friends who rarely, if ever, left their apartments, and even on the few occasions when they did, took what we considered extreme precautions, including stuffing cotton balls in their ears, and wearing hazmat suits and hospital gloves. One of my post-menopausal friends admitted to using tampons, convinced the virus could enter her body through any available opening. A couple we knew never left their home for a year, even to walk around in their own backyard. Joyce walked up and down forty-four flights of stairs to avoid her perceived risk of using the elevator. Another friend wore three masks even when she was alone in her own home.

I found myself repeating the well-regarded axiom, *let it be. Who was I to judge how others should feel?* Our response was at the other end of the spectrum, and doubtless, many of our friends did not approve of how we spent our days, out on the streets every day, interacting with homeless people. I started to wonder whether my attitude toward the pandemic was some sort of escape from the prison walls I'd created. My prison bars were not made of fear; they were made of ambition. The constant need to excel, to achieve, to be different, to win.

It had started when I'd won those first two swim races. Next, I had to get good grades. Then law school, a climb up the corporate ladder, my own law firm. Then, I became a writer. Even that wasn't enough. I applied to Columbia's MFA program, and to my surprise, I got in. For one semester, I became a student again, surrounded by other high achievers, some my age, all driven by the same hunger.

The sad truth about the need for success is that it can never be satisfied. No sooner had I achieved one milestone than I'd be planning to climb the next mountain. The need for external recognition was a relentless and insatiable master, and I was its slave.

Then, pandemic. And suddenly, I didn't have to climb anymore. On the empty streets of Manhattan, all I had to do was show up with some sandwiches. There was no ladder to climb. No prizes to win. No one to impress. I didn't even need to put on makeup. A worn-out pair of jeans and an old tee-shirt were a fine wardrobe. Every day. No one asked why I wore the same thing.

I was important only for the attention and love I showed the homeless. They didn't care about my accolades. They didn't know what kind of law I practiced, or which bylines bore my name. They only cared that we came. That we returned. That we saw them. We were just two ordinary people who they trusted.

I found myself happier and more content than I'd been in a long time. Maybe ever. It wasn't loud. It didn't sparkle. But it filled me up.

It was almost like a mathematical formula. The more I focused on others, the happier I became. That gnawing, restless need to be seen, to be applauded, to be validated, quieted. For once, I wasn't trying to make something of myself. I was just *being* and in that being I found peace.

Maybe I should not have been so surprised. When a person is trying to achieve something, they are focused on themselves, on their goals, on the hoped-for recognition and rewards they might gain by achieving them. But when we help others, we are focused on them.

It wasn't a dramatic epiphany, however. No lightning bolts. No grand realization. Just a slow, subtle unraveling of everything I thought I needed to be. A slight shift in my consciousness.

I didn't even notice it until years later when I was trying to get *Unsheltered Love* published. That old hunger came back. It strained to be noticed, to win, to succeed. And with it came the anxiety, the pressure, the whisper that I wasn't trying hard enough.

That's when it hit me. I felt the first, solid realization that during the pandemic, in the midst of the turmoil and suffering, I was *so* happy. It was almost as if I were living in an alternate universe.

By contrast, most of my friends did not seem content. Some fared better than others at enduring the prolonged shutdown. But I did not know many people who were truly happy. I never admitted how I felt at the time, not even to my family and friends, afraid they'd find fault with me for being at peace during such a difficult time for the world.

Admission or not, a crack formed in my carefully-constructed, sixty-five-year-old blueprint for success. Just a hairline fracture.

But through it—tiny at first—came an unmistakable feeling of freedom. Light flooded in, dragging an elusive truth behind it.

Somehow, that truth descended. And with every ounce of my strength, I chased it.

CHAPTER 13

D is for Danny

"If it costs you your peace, it is too expensive."
—**Paulo Coelho**

Maggie

Despite having dropped a class again, my request for tuition assistance was approved. While technically a win, it didn't feel like one. Ignoring my gut, Traci's warning, and the weight of my own exhaustion, I registered for two classes for the spring semester. I received approval for both TAP and Pell grants in the amounts of $1762 and $924, respectively, so my tuition cost was covered. Traci paid for my books. I should have felt relieved. Instead, I felt like I was balancing on the edge of something fragile, one strong gust of wind from being swept away.

I decided to celebrate by telling Traci about Danny. It wasn't a confession, it was a test. That chapter of my life is still the one of which I'm the most ashamed. I had already laid bare the darkest pieces of myself—addiction, relapses, nights I didn't know if I'd wake up. She never flinched.

But Danny? Danny was different. Danny was shame with a pulse. Even now, years later, I wear that shame like a second skin.

I think part of me wanted to push her away before she could pull me in too deep, before I started believing I deserved the kind of future she believed I could have. What does a homeless woman do with a college degree anyway? Especially one who can't even get to campus most days. I didn't want to drop out. But, just like gravity, it felt inevitable.

◆ ◆ ◆

About my relationship with Danny. How I wished D was really for Danny. It wasn't. It stood for "Destruction." "Downfall." "Despair." "Disgrace." It also translated into an F.

I'd started at Brooklyn College in September of 1999. By New Year's Eve, I was fully into the college swing. I had reconnected with my best friend from junior high, Rachel, and was spending a lot of time with Michele, the daughter of my parents' best friends.

As we welcomed the new millennium, Michele had logged into a chat room on America Online. The internet was still wild and mysterious, and chat rooms were all the rage. While I was partying the night away, Michele was striking up a conversation with a man living in Texas.

Michele was taking graduate classes at Brooklyn College, and she would often spend afternoons at our house because we lived much closer to the school than she did. It was during these afternoon visits that she first told us about the man she'd met on the internet. His name was Danny, and she was completely, madly in love with him. When she told us she'd bought him a plane ticket to visit, I was stunned. So was my mom. The year was 2000, and meeting strangers from the internet wasn't just taboo, it was dangerous. Still, curiosity buzzed through the house like static.

In February, Michele told us that the time had arrived. Danny would be flying in the following week. My mother and I anxiously awaited Michele and Danny's arrival. We could not wait to see the man who had flown all the way from Texas to meet Michele, who weighed over three hundred pounds. We left the obvious question unspoken—had Danny seen a picture of Michele?

At exactly 3:00 p.m., Michele and Danny walked into the house, and my jaw hit the floor. Into my life had arrived the most stunning man I'd ever seen. He was beautiful. Not good-looking. Not cute. Beautiful. Blond hair, piercing blue eyes, a smile that made your stomach somersault. His clothes fit perfectly, hinting at a body that made your breath catch. When he looked at me, really looked at me, something inside me twisted into knots.

Danny stayed for a week and then flew back to Texas. I thought that was the end of it. A month later, however, he was back for good. Danny and Michele were engaged, and he was moving to New York. We couldn't believe it.

Michele and Danny started coming over to the house every day. He seemed to always sit next to me, and he paid a lot more attention to me than to Michele. I should have seen it then—how wrong everything was. But I didn't. Or I wouldn't.

Nevertheless, Michele and Danny married and had a son. What none of us, including Michele, had known at the time was that the night she'd met Danny in that chat room, he'd just been released from prison earlier that day, after serving a year for robbing a deli. He came to New York and married Michele because he had nowhere else to go. Poor, unsuspecting Michele was his meal ticket. He needed a place to land. And she was soft, and sweet, and willing.

In late 2001, Danny was sent back to prison for violating his parole. While he was in jail, he sent letters and called on occasion.

He asked me to write to him and always wanted to know every-thing that was going on in my life, most important, who I was seeing and if I had a boyfriend. This continued for about a year and then stopped abruptly. I didn't really care and almost forgot he existed. With college, my job, and my social life consuming my time and money, Danny was the least of my concerns.

In 2003, Danny was released from prison for the second time and returned to New York. I saw him again at his son's birthday party. That time, our mutual attraction was no longer deniable. On the car ride home, my mother said, "Don't even think about it, Maggie." At the time, I wasn't thinking about it. Michele was my friend.

The next day, I received a call from Michele. Danny wanted to know if I could get him some weed. I, of course, said yes. We agreed to meet at Rachel's house. I arrived first and waited in the living room. A few minutes later, I heard a car horn honking. I went outside and got into Danny's car to give him the weed. When I closed the car door, we looked at each other, and the next thing I knew, his tongue was down my throat. I pushed him away, advising him never to contact me again. Nevertheless, that was the official beginning of my descent into Danny's world. I walked into the fire and didn't look back.

A few weeks later, while driving home from the grocery store, Danny told Michele he wanted a divorce. Naturally, she was heartbroken. When Michele protested, Danny became angry and started to drive erratically, causing Michele to become afraid. Due to Danny's prior criminal record, Michele obtained an order of protection, and thereafter, Danny was only allowed supervised vis-itations with his son.

Once Danny and Michele's divorce was finalized, Danny and I began to spend every possible second together. Days that I should have been in class were spent on swings, at the beach, or driving around Brooklyn. When I went to work, Danny accompanied me. All my friends knew we were together. My boss called us Bonnie and Clyde. But no one asked me why I was hanging out with my friend's ex-husband. We were reckless and delusional, living out a fantasy of love born in betrayal.

More fuel was added to our already out-of-control fire when my friend Rachel started dating Danny's best friend. Once that happened, Danny and his friend started spending the night at Rachel's apartment. Day after day, Michele asked me if I'd seen Danny around town. All the while, he was sitting next to me on the couch. For six months, we lied to everyone. Michele, my parents, friends. I was twenty. I didn't know what I was doing. Or maybe I did, and I just didn't care.

My mother told me multiple times I was playing with fire, because even though Michele and Danny's marriage was over, Michele was still in love with him. No one could believe I would hook up with Michele's ex, but at the time, I didn't see anything wrong with it. I thought Danny was fair game.

I was just a stupid kid. I was very young and foolish. It wasn't that I wanted to hurt Michele—I loved her like a sister. I just loved myself more. I was selfish and inconsiderate, and I would pay the price.

That price came in March of 2004. One morning, I was awakened by the phone ringing at 6:30 a.m. For some reason, I knew the proverbial you-know-what was about to hit the fan. I picked up the extension in my bedroom and heard Michele's hysterical voice talking to my mother on the other line.

Michele told my mother that Danny and I had been sleeping together since their divorce. Why Danny felt the need to tell her that was a mystery to me. Nevertheless, I knew things would never be the same.

I told my mother he was nuts and that he was exaggerating the nature of our relationship. My mother was horrified. I denied everything. She didn't believe a word. She said I'd ruined everything. She was right.

I dressed and left for work with a heavy heart. Danny was waiting for me when I arrived. He was excited; I was furious. He was thrilled we didn't have to hide anymore and hadn't thought about anything else.

That night, Danny went to Michele's house to visit his son in violation of the protective order, and Michele called the police. Danny was arrested and thrown in jail for the third time.

The next day, Danny called asking if I could bail him out. He gave me the address, and off I went, not considering the repercussions. I got to the courthouse and signed a $50,000 bond securing his release. He had to appear in court in six days.

We walked out of the courthouse hand-in-hand, got into my car, and then realized I had no place to take him. I came up with the genius idea that I would put him in the trunk and go home. While I was upstairs with my parents, Danny could sneak into the basement and hide until I figured out another plan.

Upon our arrival, however, my mother was waiting for me in the driveway. Michele had been notified that I'd bailed Danny out of jail. She in turn called my mother, who demanded to know where Danny was. When she insisted I open the trunk, Danny popped out like some twisted jack-in-the-box. "Hi there," he said, grinning. It wasn't funny. That was the moment I lost everything.

My mother started yelling. I told Danny to go down the block and wait on the corner while I went inside, knowing my mother would follow me. She demanded my car keys and cell phone, informing me that I had lost the right to drive my car. Grabbing my credit cards and a bag of clothes, I bolted out of there. I had no place to go, no money, and no plan. All I knew was that I was leaving with Danny.

We contacted his friend, who took us to a hotel in Rockville Centre, Long Island. We ended up in a $25-a-night hotel, eating Chinese food and pretending we were in love.

We spent our last night together at my neighbor's house. I knew something was wrong when we woke up, because Danny was acting off, but I thought it was because he was nervous about going to court. I told him not to worry—that the court would just make the restraining order permanent and tell him to stay away from Michele.

We arrived at the courthouse and sat down on a bench and waited for the bailiff to open the doors. Next, my parents arrived and sat on the bench across from us. I was shocked to see them. And more than a little nervous. *Why were they there?* The air was thick with dread. The tension was palpable. I needed to get out of there and regroup.

Just as I was about to go outside for a cigarette, Danny told me he'd lied when he said he was finished with his legal troubles. In fact, he was still on probation and had not been to see his probation officer in months. The odds were he was not going to be leaving the courthouse with me that day. My heart sank. I had no idea what I was going to do. I was furious and heartbroken, but I had no time for that. Danny was called before the judge.

The prosecutor asked for the recommended sentence—eleven months—for failure to show up at a probation meeting. Despite the prosecutor's request, the judge took it upon herself to sentence Danny, based on his record and the statement my mother gave to the court, to three years in prison. They cuffed him and led him out screaming my name and apologizing. I just sat on the hard bench like a stone. My parents came over and told me to get my things together. It was time to go home.

That car ride was the first time I ever smoked a cigarette in front of my parents. I rolled down the window and lit one up. They didn't say a word about it. They didn't say a word about anything. I think they were just so relieved Danny was out of my life. It also felt like we were all mourning someone who'd just died. It wasn't Danny. My parents would not have mourned his loss. It was their daughter. That girl was gone.

When we arrived at our house, I had to get ready for my cousin's wedding in New Orleans. We were leaving the following morning. Everyone had been worried I was not going to show up since I'd been missing for the last five days. I was given my cell phone, car keys, and a hundred dollars to get my hair and nails done.

The next day, we flew to New Orleans for my cousin's wedding. I was a bridesmaid, dressed in pretty things, moving like a ghost. I don't remember the vows, or the music, or the cake. I only remember the ache. My entire world had changed in twenty-four hours, and I had no idea how to process it, but I was beginning to understand just how badly I'd damaged my relationship with my parents.

As I look back on this unfortunate incident today, I wonder if it was the catalyst for the breakup of our family. The following year, my mother moved out of our house into an apartment a few miles away, taking two of our five cats with her. Shortly thereafter, my father moved to Florida, leaving my sister and me to fend for ourselves.

The deterioration in my parents' relationship was just the beginning of the loss. The first day we were back, I went to Rachel's house. I hadn't seen or spoken to her since I'd left her house the previous week with Danny. She, too, was furious, and it took hours for her to speak to me.

When I got home, I found my prized stuffed clown, Mr. George, ripped to shreds on my bed. That was the moment when I realized just how furious my mother was. I had irreparably damaged the relationship between our family and Michele's—a relationship that had existed for decades. Now, I would never again sit at their table for Rosh Hashanah dinner or get my presents at the annual Hanukkah party. That part of my life was lost forever.

My mother was not happy about it. I didn't blame her. I gathered up the remains of Mr. George and went downstairs to the basement, which had, until that point, been used for storage and hanging out with friends. I opened up the pull-out couch and never slept in my bedroom again, exiling myself to the basement, where I believed I belonged.

I resumed my normal "pre-Danny" life. I went back to work and back to school. I avoided Danny's calls for about two weeks, but whether or not I wanted to admit it, I missed him and wanted to hear his voice. He was locked up on Long Island but allowed visitors once a week.

The following week, I went to see him. Ironically, there was a snowstorm that day. I took a half day off work and then drove the hour to the prison. He apologized. I forgave him. Again. He was my first love. My poison. My undoing. And then, just like that, he was gone. I lost track of Danny after that day. The last I heard, he was serving time in a prison in Oklahoma.

By this point, I'd also come to the realization that I was failing out of college. I'd missed far too much work over the past six months, and there was no way I was going to pass my statistics class. Of course, I didn't tell my parents. Right up until the morning of graduation, when my dad was putting on his suit, I'd kept up the ruse.

One of the saddest moments of my life was telling my father I wasn't graduating that day. I have never forgotten the look on his face, and never will. In typical fashion, my mother yelled for days. I let her. I deserved it. Danny had destroyed my life, and I had helped him. Now what was I going to do?

What to do showed up a few months later in the form of a friend I'd known for a few years. Charlie had moved to the Poconos in Pennsylvania with his family. His father had passed away from a heart attack, his mother was extremely depressed, and Charlie was lonely. He asked me to come live with them. It seemed to me the perfect escape—run away and hide in the mountains for a while. I thought isolation would heal me. I learned the hard way that you cannot run from your own reflection.

I turned in my car, left the apartment I'd been sharing with my sister since our father had moved to Florida, and headed to Pennsylvania. Rachel was so angry with me for leaving; she didn't speak to me for a year. I didn't care. I was depressed and needed an escape.

My time in the Poconos was both peaceful and torture. Charlie was a strange bird with an odd family. In that lonely mountain house, I gained fifty pounds, smoked too much pot, and spiraled into depression. I buried myself in gardening, scrapbooking, and World of Warcraft. I was Magdalynn the Undead Priest online—powerful, respected, adored. Everything I wasn't in real life.

Apparently, I was a natural at the game. I've thought about the irony of this many times over the years. I excelled at an online fantasy game, yet I could not get my real life in order. Within a few months, I'd become a guild leader with hundreds of people under me. Charlie grew frustrated as I advanced in the game, and our relationship deteriorated as I began to spend more and more time in the online world as Magdalynn. It was during this time that I met my future husband online.

I stayed in Pennsylvania until 2007, but eventually grew antsy trapped in the mountains and decided to return to New York. Surprisingly, my mother and sister were very happy to have me back. My mother even bought me my own computer on which to play *World of Warcraft*, so I didn't have to use my sister's.

I had to get a job, so I took one as a recruiter at an executive search firm on Park Avenue. It wasn't a great job, but I stayed there for a year and was promoted twice. I was the happiest I'd been in a long time. I was finally getting back to myself. I was also in a new relationship with the man who would soon become my husband.

But my husband—a wonderful, caring, intelligent person, and an excellent father—never had a chance with me. Like Michele, I was still in love with Danny. Our marriage was doomed even before we exchanged "I do's" in the backyard of his parents' house, the sun shining, the birds chirping, masking the unhappiness yet to come. All I could think about was a man in a prison cell in Oklahoma, still whispering my name.

CHAPTER 14

Virgins and Rapes

"The wound is where the light enters you."
—Rumi

Maggie

My heart pounded against my ribs as I watched Traci's face. Unbelievably, Danny's horrific story hadn't sent her running for the hills. Her unwavering presence stirred something in me—a desperate need to test just how deep her loyalty ran. A few days later, the dark truth clawing at my chest demanded release.

One afternoon, as my complaints about my husband spilled out, Traci's patient eyes met mine. "Well," she said softly, "other than Danny and Rick, it sounds like you've actually had good luck in the men department."

Her observation unnerved me. Yes, my husband had been a devoted partner and father. William was nothing short of angelic. Out of four serious relationships, I was batting .500—a coin flip between salvation and damnation. But there was one story, one jagged, bleeding memory I'd kept hidden from Traci. And now, it demanded to be heard.

The memory floods back with brutal clarity—that miserable, rain-soaked Thursday in November. I was thirteen. My father had a volleyball game, and my mother had a doctor's appointment. Freedom beckoned, dangerous and thrilling. I still had pretty strict rules about where I could go and with whom. I told my mom I was heading to my friend's house and instead went to the pool hall.

When I walked in, I saw him. He was twenty-two and so handsome. I went to school with his younger cousins and had met him a few times before at the same pool hall. The other times he had been with his friends and family. This time he was alone. And so was I.

When he approached, his smile sent electric currents through my veins. "Hello," he said, his voice deep and smooth.

"Where are your friends?"

"They'll be along," I lied, my voice betraying my youth.

"Want to grab something to eat?" he asked. Oh, how desperately I wanted to be worthy of his attention! I happily accepted. I couldn't believe he was paying attention to me.

We walked toward the nearby Chinese restaurant and then he said he had to stop at his place to grab something. He invited me to come inside instead of standing outside in the rain. The apartment door closed behind us with a decisive click. The lock clicked as it slid into place. His lips crashed against mine before I could draw breath. My body froze, not in pleasure but in primal terror.

The living room rug scraped against my back as he threw me down. The sound of his zipper tore through the silence. My pants vanished. Three minutes—three eternal, soul-crushing minutes—that's all it took to shatter my virginity. Before reality could sink into my consciousness, he was standing, straightening his clothes, issuing commands about returning to the pool hall as if nothing had happened.

A week later, he disappeared back to Europe. I was left hollow, confused, and broken without even understanding what had been stolen from me. Months crawled by before the terrible truth dawned—I had been raped. A thirteen-year-old virgin, unaware of what violation even meant. I didn't understand then. I know better now.

As I finished pouring out my story to Traci, I shamefully realized part of me expected pity, perhaps even financial compensation for my "suffering." Instead, her eyes welled with recognition and shared pain. Traci had been date-raped in college. She'd stopped confiding in people long ago, tired of hearing, "That's not so bad." The dismissal of her trauma had forced her into silence, a prison I knew all too well.

Emboldened by our shared pain, I decided to reveal my deepest shame—the second time I'd been sexually exploited. If this confession didn't drive her away, nothing would.

Just three months after Rick and I'd arrived in New York, having learned the harsh economics of street survival, I was begging on the corner while Rick worked "the line." Across the street stood a LinkNYC device—the very same telephone I would use three years later to call my caseworker, Lina.

A handsome stranger charged his phone at the kiosk. I still had my glasses and watched him carefully, drinking in his easy confidence. An hour later, he walked away, his phone forgotten on the charging station. Without hesitation, I darted across the street, snatched the device, and tried to catch him, but he'd vanished into the faceless crowd. Minutes later, he returned frantically to the kiosk.

The relief that washed over his face when I approached with his phone quickly hardened into wariness as he noticed my panhandling cup. I had no intention of asking for payment—some small part of my soul still clung to decency.

"Wait," he called as I turned to leave. "What's your name? Mine is Toast. I don't have much money, but are you hungry? I can buy you a cheeseburger." The word "cheeseburger" awakened a gnawing emptiness in my stomach that had become my constant companion.

"I'm Maggie," I replied, hunger winning over caution. "Can I get the two for $3 deal from McDonald's?" I couldn't return to Rick empty-handed—the consequences would be too painful.

Toast handed me a ten-dollar bill, his fingers warm against my frigid hand, and crossed the street to tell Rick where I went. A few minutes later, I returned with the food and change, earning a puzzled look from Toast, who doubtless had expected me to keep the change. Such honesty was rare on the streets.

That night, as Rick and I prepared our makeshift bed, he mentioned liking Toast, explaining that he'd recently been released from jail and made his living boosting high-end merchandise. Toast's polished appearance allowed him entry to places most homeless people couldn't access. I felt a strange flutter of hope that we might see him again.

Within the hour, Toast materialized by our bedding. Rick jumped up with suspicious eagerness, and the two men walked away, locked in hushed conversation. When Rick returned, his face wore the expression I'd come to dread. "Pack up. We're leaving." Confusion and anxiety churned in my stomach.

"What do you mean? Where are we going?"

"We're going to the hotel up the street. Toast got us all a room."

Cold fear slithered down my spine. This behavior was completely out of character for Rick, who normally regarded strangers with paranoid suspicion. Something was wrong, but I gathered my belongings in silent compliance.

The hotel room was deceptively charming—clean, comfortable, with amenities I'd forgotten existed. When Rick suggested I shower, I happily embraced the rare luxury, allowing hot water to cascade over my skin for the first time in weeks.

But paradise shattered when I returned to find Toast lounging on the bed in his boxer shorts, drugs scattered across the nightstands beside neat stacks of cash. My still-wet body turned to ice as understanding dawned. Rick had sold me. Sold me for $200, drugs, and a hotel room. The transaction had been completed while I stood unknowing on our corner.

Shock, rage, and humiliation crashed through me like tidal waves. But beneath it all lay the cold certainty of my powerlessness. We were already in the room. The money had changed hands. The drugs had been consumed. Refusing would mean a beating—or worse. For the first and only time, I allowed Rick to pimp me out. The memory burns like acid, the deepest shame of my broken life. I had no idea this single night would fester like an untreated wound for years to come.

Ironically, Toast himself was gentle and considerate. I awoke the next morning with money in my pocket and unexpected warmth toward this stranger. By dawn, we'd formed a connection neither of us had anticipated, least of all Rick, who had seen me as nothing more than a commodity to be traded.

Upon returning to our corner, I assumed I'd never see Toast again. But at 3:30 that morning, a finger tapped my shoulder. There stood Toast, pressing his finger to his lips in a silent plea for discretion.

Rick didn't stir as I slipped away. Down the street, Toast embraced me with unexpected tenderness, giving me the sweetest kiss. He pressed $50 into my palm and whispered, "Don't tell Rick. Use the money for yourself."

With one final kiss, he disappeared into the night, leaving me standing alone with hidden money and a heart confused by conflicting emotions.

The next morning at Starbucks, Toast appeared again, his face lighting up at the sight of me. "How do you like your coffee?" he asked, his voice warm with genuine interest.

When Rick entered minutes later and found us sharing coffee, his roar of jealousy shattered the brief moment of peace. I abandoned my drink and Toast, dragging Rick outside with desperate explanations.

Rick's fist connected with my face before I could finish speaking. But this time, Toast witnessed everything. In a blur of movement, he chased Rick around a parked car and, with one swift motion, tore Rick's arm from its socket. Rick collapsed, clutching his useless limb. When I rushed to help him, he pushed me away with a stream of familiar abuse before limping toward the hospital. Toast approached me, his voice impossibly gentle after such violence. "Shall we finish that cup of coffee?"

I returned to my corner and awaited Rick's return. An hour later, arm in a sling, Rick approached with venomous satisfaction.

"Looking for someone? Don't worry; you won't be able to see him anymore."

He yanked my glasses off my face and threw them to the ground, crushing them beneath his heel. Three years would pass before I saw the world clearly again.

Nevertheless, from that day forward, Toast became my unlikely guardian angel, somehow appearing whenever danger loomed. I grew to adore him, and everyone knew it, especially Rick. Toast was my knight in shining armor in a world where fairy tales had long ago turned to nightmares.

When I finished my story, Traci's mouth hung open in stunned silence. "Wow," she finally whispered. "I cannot even imagine someone doing that to me."

"I was shocked," I admitted, the pain still raw despite the passage of time. "Rick is so jealous by nature that it caught me completely off guard that he would voluntarily pimp me out."

Traci's eyes glistened with tears. "So between us," she said, her voice breaking, "we have child rape, date rape, and pimp rape."

"Which is worse?" I asked, the question hanging heavy between us.

"Rape is rape," Traci answered, her voice suddenly stronger. "I guess I should tell you my story."

"Maybe another day," I suggested gently. Traci was already crying, her shoulders shaking with the weight of unspoken memories.

The following week, Traci finally shared her own nightmare—a college sophomore at nineteen, accepting a date with a popular senior fraternity president. What should have been a magical homecoming night turned into horror when a private moment upstairs spiraled into violent assault.

"I could hear everyone partying in the living room downstairs," she recalled, her voice hollow with remembered terror. "I was in an alternate universe."

Like my own experience at thirteen, it ended before she could fully comprehend what had happened. "I just got up, pulled my skirt down, and, leaving my underwear on the floor, ran out of the frat house. I did not stop until I got back to my dorm."

The next day, Traci confided in her roommate, Therese, only to have her story dismissed as exaggeration. The final, cruel twist came two weeks later when Therese accepted a date with the same man and returned as a victim herself. He had raped her, too.

Our scars, different yet born of the same violence, bound us together in a sisterhood neither of us had ever wanted to join.

Awake

> *"One day you will tell the story of how you overcame what you went through, and it will become someone else's survival guide."*
> —**Brené Brown**

CHAPTER 15

Civil Disobedience

"Awakening is not changing who you are
but discarding who you are not."
—**Deepak Chopra**

Traci

By Christmas of 2022, Maggie and I were in constant communication. Our phones buzzed with messages and calls—discussions about her school assignments flowing seamlessly into worried exchanges about health. Each notification that lit up my screen took me back to that pivotal moment when I'd first given her my email, never realizing where that small gesture would lead.

◆ ◆ ◆

The summer of 2020 hung heavy with uncertainty when I created that second email account. My fingers hesitated over the keyboard as I sent her the new email in case of an emergency. I never expected her to use it, but an emergency arrived less than a week later when a barrage of frantic messages filled my inbox.

I knew something was wrong. That was saying a lot, because in Maggie's world, almost everything was perpetually wrong.

I didn't have time to reply. Joel and I were helping our son, Chad, who'd called in the middle of the night asking us to come to his apartment. We found him in bed, curled in a fetal position. We convinced ourselves it was just food poisoning from his take-out dinner—a comforting lie to keep the fear at bay as we watched over him until morning.

When his symptoms grew more severe, we did what every parent dreads—especially during the early months of the pandemic—we called 911. An ambulance arrived in less than two minutes.

I stood on the empty sidewalk as they took him away, the distance between us growing with every second. The cruel reality of pandemic protocols meant neither Joel nor I could accompany him to the hospital. Like countless others during that year, Chad was on his own.

Two hours later, Chad called with an update. He sounded brave, but I knew he was scared. He had acute pancreatitis and needed emergency surgery to remove a stone blocking the duct connecting his gallbladder to his pancreas.

I finally responded to Maggie's barrage of messages with the stark simplicity of my own crisis: *Chad is in the hospital. Talk later.* "Later" arrived less than an hour later when a series of further messages revealed that Maggie was in her own heightened state of panic. Oddly, none of this seemed so unusual. Panic was everywhere in summer of 2020.

Unable to help Chad and desperate to do something useful, I headed downtown to Maggie's corner. She spotted me from two blocks away, her face lighting with relief as she ran toward me, her worn sneakers slapping against the pavement.

"I'm so sorry to bother you" she said, eyes wide with concern despite her own obvious distress. "I know you have your hands full with Chad, but I need you!"

"What's happened now?"

"Rick's been arrested. The police took him to jail."

"What did he do this time?"

"He hit a man with a pipe."

The news didn't shock me, but my stomach still twisted with the memory of Rick's pipe whistling through the air toward us during a recent conversation with Maggie. The terror of that moment had sent me running so abruptly that I'd lost a shoe, forced to walk home barefoot across New York's unforgiving pavement. New York City is no place for walking around without shoes. I was not happy.

Maggie had no way of raising bail money, and although afraid of being alone, she was secretly relieved at the temporary reprieve from Rick's fists. Even Rick's mother had very little to say and no money to offer for bail when Maggie called to inform her that her son was in jail again.

"He's better off in jail than on the street—go enjoy yourself for a change," she said, the click of the phone echoing her indifference.

The following night, William appeared on the scene with the flourish of the proverbial prince on a white horse intent on saving the damsel in distress. A charismatic Black man who'd befriended Maggie the previous year, William had never crossed the boundary from friend to lover. But Rick was now in jail, and William invited Maggie to share a picnic dinner. As they dined by the East River under an array of stars, William worked his magic, and his gentle charm melted away years of defensive barriers. By night's end, Maggie had discovered something she'd forgotten existed—tenderness.

When I saw Maggie the following day, I winked and said, "William just told us you two had a good time last night."

"I sure did, Tray," she said, using the nickname she'd given me. "And it was so nice to have someone treat me well for a change."

Unlike the other homeless people we knew, William had secured a foothold on stability with a safe haven room. Days after Rick's arrest, however, William won what many considered impossible—the homeless lottery of permanent housing. He was the first—and still the only—homeless person we've known to transition from temporary to permanent housing. William was on top of the world—a new girlfriend and a new home.

But even fairy tales have their complications. William was required to quarantine in his safe haven room for fourteen days to prove he was COVID-free. For a man who had spent years behind bars, the requirement wasn't just inconvenient—it was psychologically unbearable.

"I just can't be locked up again," he admitted. "No matter what the cost. I've been in and out of prison or juvenile detention centers since I was fifteen."

"Do you have a better plan?" Joel asked.

"I always have a better plan," Civil replied with a mischievous smile.

Rebellious by nature, William could not follow rules, even as a child. He'd started his lifelong tendency to steal by helping himself to candy and soda pop at the bodegas in his New Jersey neighborhood. As he grew, so did his infractions. Candy turned into beer, which eventually led to cash to buy drugs. And then, following the sudden passing of his mother due to an asthma attack, circumstances rapidly deteriorated. William was fourteen years old.

William's father had died the year before, and he was convinced that his mother's new boyfriend had hidden her inhaler. At her funeral, William, overcome with grief, tried to take his mother's body out of the casket. He was restrained and then hospitalized. It was the beginning of a long descent into darkness that would transcend far more than the numerous prison cells he would encounter.

The year before we'd met him, William had moved to New York City on a whim. "I just heard an inner voice telling me to come here. I had nothing left in New Jersey, and I thought a new place would help break the endless cycle of incarcerations and releases," he said. Hope glimmered in his voice whenever he spoke of that decision, perhaps the first time he'd truly chosen his own path.

When William arrived in New York, he set up a makeshift home on 32nd Street atop a subway grate that blew hot air in the winter and cool air in the summer. The following year, he was placed in a series of safe haven rooms, none of which worked out because he couldn't get along with his roommates.

Discouraged, but not defeated, he registered with a different agency. His first placement with that agency was likewise a failure. For six long months, he'd drifted between bank vestibules and subway cars, one of many homeless people living in the city's forgotten shadows.

Learning the significance of William's housing offer prompted us to research the Byzantine process of homeless housing. As coveted as a safe haven room is, being assigned permanent housing is a whole new level of housing security. It also represents a first step toward meaningful reintegration into society. With shelter and utilities provided, and food stamps available to cover basic nutritional needs, the next step is finding employment. William stood at the threshold of transformation, with only the quarantine requirement blocking his way.

With the silver-tongued persuasion that had become his survival tool, William convinced his caseworker to accept three negative COVID tests instead of a quarantine. William had also used his charms to work his way up the list for permanent housing by checking himself into Bellevue and convincing the doctors he had a mental illness. If he did have one, I never saw any evidence of it except that William drank. And smoked K2. Nevertheless, William was certified with a mental illness, thus ensuring a high priority on the waiting list. In June, with Maggie by his side, William moved into his first permanent housing in Brooklyn.

Meanwhile, the city remained in suspended animation, its residents tracking daily death counts with morbid vigilance. As virus numbers began their tentative decline, New Yorkers stirred with cautious hope. Governor Cuomo announced the reopening schedule, phase one beginning June 8th. Not much changed, however, until restaurants were allowed to reopen on June 22, the date phase two began.

The pandemic had negatively impacted on the restaurant industry with merciless efficiency. In our neighborhood alone, over half the establishments had surrendered to economic reality, including the local diner that had served generations for seven decades. But those who survived transformed the cityscape with stunning resilience. Seemingly overnight, makeshift patios blossomed into enchanting outdoor venues that evoked European cafés rather than pandemic compromises.

The timing was as perfect as the weather. Dry, hot days cooled off at night, and the outdoor dining venues, twinkling with lights, provided a bustling, lively atmosphere throughout the city. Hope reappeared in an otherwise shuttered and depressed environment, and for the first time in months, I noticed smiling faces, albeit hidden behind masks. Nevertheless, there was a palpable optimism in the air, breathing life into a city that had already lost thousands of its residents to the virus, with thousands more lives hanging in the balance.

Though I've never experienced war firsthand, New York in that moment resembled scenes from countless films—a war-ravaged city whose shell-shocked inhabitants had just received news of peace. The devastation remained visible in boarded storefronts and missing faces, yet slowly, cautiously, people emerged from their shelters. Stores raised their shutters, restaurants welcomed servers back, and hair salons formed lines that stretched down blocks, filled with New Yorkers in desperate need of haircuts.

Despite the dire predictions, New York State continued to beat the odds. *The New York Times* reported the surprising facts—only one percent of the 30,000 COVID tests being administered each day were positive. The low incidence was in sharp contrast to other large cities.

For Maggie and William, summer 2020 passed in relative tranquility, disturbed only by occasional sightings of Rick, who had gained release in July after a social service agency posted his bail. September brought Maggie's thirty-ninth birthday; William turned forty-three. Young by some measures, ancient by others, housed and in love, they drifted through those golden months watching in wonder as the city—once deemed the most dangerous place on earth—slowly reclaimed its pulse.

As Maggie reveled in Brooklyn's autumn splendor and the unprecedented luxury of safety in the arms of a man who treated her with genuine tenderness, she remained oblivious to the storm clouds gathering on distant horizons. She couldn't know that her father in Florida was showing the first ominous signs of declining health, or that her estranged parents would soon reunite in New York. What she did begin to sense, however, with the instinct of someone long accustomed to reading danger signals, was that something was wrong with William.

Maggie was soon to learn that the refuge she found in William had an expensive price tag. Yet, even as unseen threats gathered force, she doubled down on rebuilding her life, clinging to her fragile new beginning with fierce determination. Standing at the crossroads of hope and heartbreak, Maggie remained unaware of the gathering darkness, its shadow already stretching toward the light she had only just discovered.

CHAPTER 16

Sheltered at Last

"You are not the darkness you endured.
You are the light that refused to surrender."
—John Mark Green

Maggie

For the first time in what felt like forever, I was safe. The realization washed over me in waves. Sometimes they were gentle waves, like the ones that lulled me to sleep on that beach in Atlantic City. Sometimes they were overwhelmingly deafening. I was sheltered not just by walls and a roof, but by William's love. A love that asked for nothing in return that expected no payment of flesh or dignity. A love that felt so strange it sometimes frightened me more than Rick's fists ever had.

Maggie feeling happy

Nevertheless, I found myself waiting for the other shoe to drop. My body reacted with tension to abrupt movements, and my shoulders would instinctively hunch in response to even a slight elevation in someone's voice. Rick had altered my nervous system to connect tenderness with danger and view kindness as a precursor to unrest. He'd trained me to flinch at gentle touches and to second guess softness.

I'd come to believe that love always came with a price, to accept bruises, broken bones, and tears cried silently into pillows. So even with William, whose eyes held nothing but kindness when they looked at me, my heart sometimes braced for the worst, like a dog who's been kicked too many times to trust a gentle hand.

William's health was deteriorating in ways that frightened me. Although I didn't know what was wrong, I knew what was happening. He started to have seizures. Just little ones at first. A few seconds when he would grow quiet and check out. I became afraid to leave him alone. I couldn't bear the thought of him seizing on the floor with no one to cradle his head, to whisper that everything would be okay. Georgia anticipated every seizure and when it was over, she comforted him. But she couldn't call 911 or take care of him when I wasn't there.

Through all of that, my heart ached with a different kind of pain when I thought about my parents. Five years. The thought of seeing them ignited joy—they were returning to New York that fall. Yet, while there was hope that fluttered like a trapped bird, there was also dread that sat heavy in my stomach. I missed them with a physical ache that sometimes woke me up at night.

Part of me longed to show them the new version of myself. I was stronger, steadier than the last time they'd seen me, healed despite the scars that mapped my journey. But there was another part of me that carried the weight of shame, which was suffocating. Would they forgive my disappearance? Would they see in my eyes the things I'd done to survive and turn away in disgust? Would they identify me as their daughter or simply acknowledge me as someone familiar from the past?

The biggest fear of all, though, was my father. My hero since childhood. My rock when the world felt too big and too cruel. The man who had never let me down, not even once, who taught me that men could be gentle and strong at the same time. I didn't know if my heart—scarred and patched together as it was—could bear to see him frail, to witness his decline into someone who needed me as much as I had once needed him. That kind of role reversal felt like a heartbreak too heavy to carry, a fundamental shift in the laws of the universe.

Boarding the Staten Island Ferry that fall morning felt like stepping onto an emotional tightrope strung across an abyss. That small strip of water felt like an ocean. As we passed the Statue of Liberty with her torch raised defiantly against the sky, I thought of the millions of immigrants who had crossed oceans for a second chance, who'd left everything behind for the promise of something better. I wondered if they felt as unsure as I did that day. Would they have been torn between past and present, guilt and gratitude, between who they had been and who they now were?

When I walked through my parents' front door, everything paused. Time didn't seem to matter. Their smiles were the same ones I remembered, and they wrapped around me like the warmest blanket on the coldest night. My father was slower, his movements more delicate, but his eyes still crinkled at the corners the way they always had when he looked at me. He was still my dad. My mother's hands, soft with age now, touched my face like she was memorizing it, as if she feared I might disappear if she blinked.

We laughed, talked, and hugged like time had only bent, not broken. My mother was the same. Her face, which had always hardened slightly at my rebellions, softened when she looked at me now, as if my absence had washed away all the small resentments, leaving only the love beneath. That moment was a small miracle, a gift I wasn't sure I deserved but accepted with gratitude. I left their house that day with tears streaming down my face. I was relieved, overwhelmed, and cautiously hopeful. We were rebuilding.

With all the joy that day there was still one absence that clanged in the room louder than words, one empty chair at the table that seemed to scream with silence. My sister refused to see me, though she lived only five minutes away. I understood her anger, and I respected it. I'd vanished from her life without explanation, without goodbye. I'd left a crater in her life, a Maggie-shaped hole that had hardened over time into bitterness. I didn't blame her. I just missed her with an ache that felt physical, like a phantom limb pain.

William's health continued to deteriorate and left me emotionally wrung out. Then the diagnosis came, delivered in a sterile dark room by a doctor who couldn't quite meet our eyes. Epilepsy. William's seizures, which were violent, terrifying episodes that turned the man I loved into a stranger thrashing on the floor finally had a name. Unfortunately, that name didn't come with the answers we desperately needed. It came with tests, pills, and uncertainty.

The seizures continued, indifferent to medication and to my desperate bargaining with a God I wasn't sure I believed in anymore. Each one took more of him from me, erased another small part of the man whose quiet strength had saved me in more ways than he would ever know. I remembered the first sign that showed up months before the pandemic turned the world upside down, when everything still felt survivable, when the worst thing I could imagine was another night with Rick's hands around my throat.

◆◆◆

It was a very cold winter night, with temperatures that turned breath into visible vapor and made individuals without shelter gather closer for warmth despite potential risks. Rick shook me awake roughly, his fingers digging into my shoulder hard enough to leave five perfect bruises by morning. He ordered me to Madison Square Garden to get K2—that synthetic marijuana that is cheaper, stronger, and infinitely more dangerous than the real thing. I didn't want to go. I was still new to the streets and terrified to walk alone so late. But the alternative was much worse. Rick's unpredictable rage, his creative punishments that left wounds no one could see. I rose from the unclean mattress, dressed in all available layers of clothing, and proceeded on my way.

The heating grate remained memorable. Steam rising around a circle of people gathered there for warmth. This grate was well known even to "newbies" because when it rained it blew so much heat that the rain evaporated before it could hit the ground. A man sitting slightly apart called out my name, his voice somehow familiar though I couldn't place it. I turned, confused and wary.

"It's me, William," he said, and though his face remained a stranger's, something in his eyes sparked recognition. I didn't remember him, but he remembered me. He handed me my first blunt of K2, his fingers briefly touching mine. That night's connection changed everything, though I understood its impact later.

William became a daily presence in my strange, new world. When Rick wasn't around he'd smoke with me, talk with me, listen to me. Really listen, as if my words mattered, as if I mattered. That alone set him apart in a world where people barely saw each other, where eye contact was either a challenge or an invitation, never just acknowledgment of shared humanity.

William saw me and not the shell I'd become. He saw the person still fighting to exist beneath the layers of trauma and shame. As we shared more stories, more quiet moments watching the city move around us, our connection deepened into something neither of us had words for yet. We were two broken people who found comfort in each other's cracks, whose jagged edges somehow fit together to create something almost whole.

I still laugh about the toothbrush story. William left his apartment for good one day because his roommate used his toothbrush without asking. I didn't have a toothbrush back then. Basic hygiene was a luxury beyond my reach, something I dreamed about along with hot showers and clean sheets. But I admired him for it. That conviction, that quiet dignity that refused to be compromised, even when compromise might have meant a roof over his head. Toothbrush became our secret code word for enough. A warning signal that a boundary had been crossed. It was the first time I'd considered that I might deserve boundaries too, that there might be lines no one should be allowed to cross with me.

When William disappeared for a few days and came back with a neck brace, his movements stiff and somewhat changed, I didn't know how serious his injury was. I didn't know that the sidewalk that he had fallen on was the beginning of something far more dangerous than a simple loss of balance.

Life kept moving at its relentless pace. Then, Rick got arrested with my benefit card in his pocket, my only legitimate source of food. I walked alone across town terrified with each block. I didn't know this side of town. I was hesitant and nervous and then literally bumped into William. Of all the blocks in New York City, all the street corners and bodega entrances where I might have paused. The mathematical odds against it seemed impossible, but it happened, and it felt right.

That same night, with the sky turning purple above us, William asked me on our first date. A picnic by the East River, bodega sandwiches and a small bottle of booze, moonlight dancing on the water like strings of silver. For the first time in years, I felt something bloom in my chest that I barely recognized as hope.

That was our beginning. It wasn't fancy or conventional. It was not the stuff of romantic comedies or love songs. Even though we were still homeless, still fighting each day for basic survival, I felt something I'd forgotten existed. William protected me without controlling me. He cherished me without possessing me. After years with Rick, that distinction was revolutionary and earth-shattering in its simplicity.

But as we all know, love isn't always simple, especially not when it grows between two people living on society's edges. William stole to survive. We both did. Only small things and only from stores. His go-to was Ensure, the meal replacement drink, which he stole from pharmacies and sold for twenty bucks a pack in Harlem. Every time he went "to work," my heart lodged in my throat. If he got caught, I'd lose him and my newfound home, fragile as it was. Still, hunger makes a thief of the most decent people. And while I hated the danger, I understood the desperation that drove him, the primal need to provide that had been wired into him by a society that simultaneously demanded strength from men and then criminalized the lengths they went to when showing it when conventional ways were no longer an option.

Eventually, I begged him to stop. The constant fear was fueling my imagination, painting vivid pictures of him in handcuffs, of visiting rooms with bulletproof glass between us, of years stretching before me where I was alone again. All it took was for me to say the words. He stopped not with anger or defensiveness. Not with blame or accusations. He just listened and somehow heard the fear beneath my words. That's who William was. That's who he still is, even as his health betrays him. He is someone who listens to what I'm really saying, even when I don't have the right words.

Then came a major seizure. It struck like lightning from the sky on a clear day. William frozen mid-sentence, eyes rolling back, then convulsing with a violence that seemed impossible from his gentle frame, blood staining his lips where he'd bitten his tongue. I held him while I waited for the ambulance, shaking as much as he was, whispering desperate promises and prayers into his unhearing ears. No one can put into words the terror of watching someone you love fall apart in your arms. How it feels to be completely powerless to help them. It is something that carves itself into your soul and doesn't leave. It just waits, patiently, ready to resurface in your nightmares.

After that seizure, he was never quite the same. Something had shifted. There was a new hesitancy, a wariness, as if he no longer trusted his own body. Despite the medications that dulled his quick wit and bright spirit, the seizures increased in frequency, duration, and strength. Each one dimmed his light a little more, took another small piece of the man I'd once known.

◆ ◆ ◆

Amidst all of William's medical crises and appointments that fall, the school semester continued in a blur of missed classes and sympathetic emails from professors. Though my body and mind craved rest; a real rest, not the hypervigilant half-sleep I'd grown accustomed to, it was not to be.

In addition to William's deteriorating health, my father, also, was fading faster than anyone had anticipated, his brilliant mind clouding over with increasing frequency. My sister and mother, finally acknowledging they couldn't manage alone anymore, asked me to move into my parents' house to help care for my dad.

I wanted to say yes with my whole heart. I needed to be there, to store up memories before there were no more to be made. But that move meant stepping away from school the next semester, from the dream of graduation I'd fought so hard to achieve. Still, in the end, I said yes. Because I loved my father. And after years of abuse and isolation, after giving pieces of myself away until I barely recognized what was left, love meant more than any degree ever could.

Nevertheless, while sacrificing school was an easy decision, leaving William alone was not. The choice split me in two. I watched helplessly as William's seizures grew more violent and more frequent. The medication wasn't saving him. It was killing him slowly, turning him into a ghost with vacant eyes and sluggish movements. The problem was that stopping the medication might kill him, too.

I lived in a fog of impossible choices, of competing needs that all felt urgent and necessary. I was afraid to lose William to his broken brain or the depression that increasingly kept him in bed, afraid to lose my dad to the disease stealing him piece by piece, afraid to lose myself in the tide of caregiving that threatened to drown my own identity, my own dreams. There were no right answers. Just love, and the weight it carried, both burden and blessing.

But love, too, is a kind of shelter. More permanent than bricks, more waterproof and solid than any roof. And no matter how fragile it sometimes felt, it was mine. Built with my own hands, my own heart. After everything I had been through. After Rick's brutality, after cold nights under scaffolding, after hunger and fear and degradation, I had created something beautiful. I had somehow found a way to make myself a home.

It was not a place but a feeling. The feeling of being truly seen, truly known, and cherished, anyway. I had learned that was the greatest shelter of all.

CHAPTER 17

The Power of Words

"The best years of your life are the ones in which
you decide your problems are your own."
—Albert Ellis

Traci

While Maggie struggled with William's seizures and her father's deteriorating health, I struggled to get our first book, *Unsheltered Love,* published. From the start, it had been a bumpy journey, involving dozens of rejections and even more drafts. Little had I known when I'd first decided to write the story that my decision would lead to the uncovering of a secret, the first of many that would cause a shift in my relationship with Maggie, and even more importantly, in my consciousness.

◆ ◆ ◆

I'd decided to write *Unsheltered Love* about a year after meeting Maggie. Because she knew so much about the subject of homelessness, I wanted to offer her a job as my developmental editor. Before doing so, however, I called her mother to discuss my plan.

Maggie's mother answered, her voice warm but weary, and skipping the perfunctory greetings, I jumped right in. "I'm thinking about writing another book and considering offering Maggie a job as a developmental editor. She seems well-read, and she does have a college degree, so I'm assuming she can work on written materials. What do you think about—?"

Her mother interrupted before I could finish my sentence.

"Traci, Maggie does not have a college degree."

"What? Maggie told me she has a graduate degree in psychology."

Maggie's mother laughed so loudly I thought she might pee her pants.

"A graduate degree?" she asked in disbelief. "No, Maggie does not have a graduate degree. In fact, she dropped out of college in her senior year."

"Why would she do that?"

"A boy—the scum of the earth. She spent all her time with him. When she flunked her statistics class, she just gave up."

I already knew about Danny, so I figured he was the boy being referenced, but hearing him described as scum of the earth made my heart ache for the younger Maggie, chasing love at the expense of her future.

"That's really too bad," I said. "She is so smart and very well-read." My throat constricted as conflicting emotions battled within me. The betrayal of Maggie's lie mingled with compassion for her shame.

"You're right about that." Pride crept into her mother's tone, a flicker of light in the darkness.

"And she was almost finished. As you said, Maggie is a voracious reader and an excellent writer. She should have studied literature, but she wanted to study psychology."

"Do you think she could do a good job working as my developmental editor, anyway?" I asked, attempting to hide my discomfort over what I'd just learned.

"Yes, Traci," her mother sighed, tired from years of hoping for her daughter's redemption. "I believe she would do a good job with an assignment like that."

Comforted by the reassurance, and despite my unease about Maggie having lied about her schooling, the next morning when I ran into her, I spoke to her about the book.

"I'm thinking about writing a book about homelessness and the pandemic. Would you like to work on it?"

"Yes!" she shouted, her face illuminated with such pure, childlike, joy that tears pricked at my eyes. She began jumping up and down, her enthusiasm bursting forth like water from a broken dam.

For the following year, Maggie and I worked on the book. Despite the increasing demands on Maggie, we somehow found the time to finish the first draft, prepare a book proposal, and submit it to our agent, who was one of the best in the industry. She submitted it to dozens of publishers, and I think we all expected multiple offers.

Then came the rejections. Thirty-five, almost all for the same reason—no one wanted to hear about homelessness from a privileged white woman. When I called Maggie to give her the bad news, expecting to hear disappointment mirroring my own, her voice carried something else entirely—determination.

"We need to rethink this," she said, her quiet confidence steadying me through the phone. "It's not just your story to tell. It's mine too."

Those words changed everything. We returned to the manuscript with renewed purpose, weaving Maggie's perspective throughout, her journal entries following each chapter. That draft met with approval.

Maggie became my co-author, writing under her pen name, a shield protecting her vulnerability from the world's harsh gaze. When *Unsheltered Love* was finally published, becoming a *Wall Street Journal* and *USA Today* bestseller, I felt something shift between us. The mentor-mentee dynamic dissolved, replaced by something richer, more equal.

But it wasn't until the book was shortlisted for the Eric Hoffer Award grand prize—one of the most prestigious awards for indie publishers—that I knew we'd created something special. When I called to tell Maggie the good news, the energy in our relationship shifted once again.

"We shouldn't expect to win," I warned her.

"Why not?" Why shouldn't *Unsheltered Love* win?"

I didn't know whether to laugh or cry. "There's only one winner out of thousands of entrants," I explained. "Only one."

Again, she repeated, "Why not us?"

I had no answer. Why shouldn't our book win? Right then and there the mystery of my beautiful—yet, at times, tortured—life came into focus. Despite a lifetime of blaming my mother when things did not work out as I had planned, none of it was her fault, and very little even had anything to do with her.

◆◆◆

Maggie's father's health continued to deteriorate. At the end of 2022, Maggie made the decision to move into her parents' house to help. Registration for the spring 2023 semester opened, and Maggie struggled to find an online class she could take while she lived in Staten Island, her shoulders heavy with the impossible weight of it all. I could tell that Maggie wanted to take the spring semester off, but true to my form, I pushed her to sign up for a class.

That night, my mother "visited" again, her presence filling my darkened bedroom like a fragrance from another time. All she said was, "Traci, don't do to Maggie what you have done to yourself." She didn't need to say more. My entire life had been a relentless pursuit of external validation and achievements that could never fill the hollow spaces within.

Flooded with the same type of embarrassment I'd felt when I first realized that it had never occurred to me to question how the homeless accomplished basic activities such as using the bathroom or washing their clothes, at least I realized that Maggie trying to take care of her father while keeping up with her school assignments would not be easy. Nevertheless, I ignored my own revelation, as well as my mother's warning, continuing to nudge Maggie toward a path that might break her.

That winter brought a series of contradictions—the heart-wrenching challenge of health scares and Maggie's academic struggles playing alongside the triumphant harmony of our book's success. Through it all, something profound blossomed between us. Maggie had become one of my best friends. *How was this possible?* I'm picky when it comes to girlfriends and have had very few in my life. At the time, I only had a handful, two of whom were my daughter and my cousin. Yet somehow, this woman— younger, from a different world, carrying burdens I could scarcely imagine—had slipped past every defense.

But even more astonishing was the truth that followed. Despite all odds, despite every reason to maintain professional distance, despite the complications and the messiness and the pain, I loved her. Not as a protégé or a project or a character in my story, but as a soul that somehow mirrored my own, though our reflections looked nothing alike.

And in that love—imperfect, unexpected, unplanned—I finally found something no achievement could ever provide: the courage to face myself.

CHAPTER 18

My Sister

"Conquer yourself rather than the world."
—René Descartes

Maggie

The fall semester ended. I signed up for one online class for the spring semester. After Christmas, with a heart both heavy and hopeful, I packed up my books and clothes, strapped Georgia into her carrier, and headed for the Staten Island ferry. The cold winter wind whipped against my face as I stood on deck, but I barely felt it. My mind was consumed with what lay ahead and the promise I was made to myself. I would be there for my father as he had always been for me.

While I desperately wanted to help, the sacrifices were not insignificant. School had to be scaled back to just one online class. My job, a rare treasure I'd discovered through the Authors Guild online discussion group, hung by a thread. Several days each week, I was a personal assistant to an elderly woman whose wealth was matched only by her eccentricity.

Her penthouse apartment overlooked Washington Square Park, where she would often sit in her large bay window, surveying her kingdom. I edited her memoirs one moment and arranged her travel needs the next, all while she paid me handsomely for tasks that felt more like privilege than work. The thought of losing that job was upsetting.

But the most gut-wrenching consideration was William's health, which had continued to spiral downward despite an arsenal of medical interventions. I took my role as William's protector with a ferocity that surprised even me. It was not just because I felt indebted to him for saving me when no one else would, but, selfishly, also because my housing depended on him.

The truth clawed at my conscience. If something happened to William, I would be cast back into the streets. Despite living in the shadowlands of homelessness for years, the system had still denied me my own permanent housing, and I'd long since lost my safe haven room at The Travelers.

William stood as the miraculous exception. He was still the only person I knew who had managed to secure his own permanent place. Many of our homeless friends had remained in temporary accommodations.

I knew William was still capable of basic self-care, but the thought of him seizing alone, vulnerable and afraid, tortured me. The decision tore me apart. My father's deterioration pulled me one way, and my obligation to William yanked me in another. Both men had thrown me lifelines when I was drowning. How could I possibly choose which one to serve now? Nevertheless, the most urgent person in need at the time was my father.

When I first moved into my parents' home, my father could still assist with his own care, his dignity somewhat intact. All too soon, however, I watched helplessness creep into his eyes. "I'm sorry, Maggie," he would say whenever I had to change him after an accident. The fact that he'd once changed my diapers did little to alleviate the discomfort we both felt when I had to change his.

I fought back with humor, desperate to preserve the last shreds of his dignity. And despite the heartbreak, I cherished those winter days with a ferocity that surprised me. He was still "with it" enough to find joy in small pleasures. We'd stay up late, like conspirators against time itself, watching concert videos on YouTube, indulging in rainbow cookies and ice pops like children stealing moments of sweetness.

I spoiled him with food, as if perfect meals could somehow heal his failing body. The refrigerator overflowed with his favorite foods. This was not just nutrition but offerings of devotion. Those first months together became a sacred gift. We made up for lost time, and wounds that had festered began to heal. We didn't need grand adventures; we never even left the house. But we were together, and that singular truth became the axis around which my world revolved.

One night, I decided to sleep on the couch beside my father. He'd fallen asleep in his recliner, the light of the television washing over his peaceful face, muttering fragmented memories. I lay there, every muscle tense, one ear straining for any change in his breathing, the other partially alert in case the first failed in its vigilance. As I hovered between wakefulness and dreaming, childhood memories flooded back.

◆ ◆ ◆

It was June 17, 2002. I'd worked until noon. At exactly 12:00 p.m., my dad and sister arrived, and we raced to the airport, carrying nothing but our small bags and one-way tickets to Ohio. My sister and I boarded the plane to Columbus, giggling like schoolgirls. When we arrived, we transferred to a small plane, seating only twenty people. The precariousness of it heightened our adventure.

When we landed in Cuyahoga Falls, my cousin Peter was waiting for us, his familiar smile a comfort in unfamiliar territory. He drove us deep into the woods, up a winding one-way trail that seemed to lead nowhere and everywhere at once. Our destination: the Blossom Music Center. To me, it was paradise disguised as the middle of nowhere. My sister had won two front-row seats for a Dave Matthews concert, and we were determined to go regardless of the distance, cost, or practicality.

We arrived at the gate breathless and found our seats just as the opening band took the stage, which went exactly according to our plan. We knew Dave always introduced the band members, and at precisely 7:00 p.m., he emerged, exactly as we knew he would! We leapt to our feet, screaming his name. He stopped mid-stride, eyes finding ours in the crowd, and walked directly over, laughter spilling from him.

"The two sisters. Really? In Cuyahoga Falls! What are you two doing here?" The fact that Dave Matthews recognized us and knew who we were filled our hearts with joy.

"We're trying to put your girls through college!" I shouted back. Dave's laughter grew harder, his head thrown back in genuine amusement, before he continued with the show. We collapsed back into our seats, exchanging glances of pure, unfiltered joy.

Afterward, my cousin drove us back to New York so I could be at work the following morning. I arrived exhausted but happy. That day remains crystallized in my memory as the single best day I've ever spent with my sister. Though I cannot remember a world without her in it, this was the first time we truly existed as friends, not just siblings bound by blood.

That concert was the culmination of our intertwined lives. I had adored my sister from the very first moment I laid eyes on her tiny form. She arrived in the world when I was two years and eight months old, and the memory of my parents bringing her home from the hospital remains vivid. Her head was covered with black curls, and she looked exactly like my cherished cabbage patch doll. I took this coincidence as divine confirmation of our connection.

Later that night, after my mother put her to bed, I crept into her room and climbed into her crib. Somehow, I lifted her tiny body in my own tiny arms and proudly carried her into the living room where my parents sat, oblivious to the theft occurring under their roof.

"My baby," I declared, my voice small but filled with fierce ownership. Looking back, those two words contained a prophecy I couldn't possibly understand.

My parents leapt up, rescuing my sister from what they assumed was a certain disaster. But that moment set the pattern for decades to come. Until homelessness tore us apart, I had carried my baby sister both literally and figuratively through our lives.

Growing up, we shared a closeness that defined us both. We wore matching outfits, our identities so intertwined that the neighbors sometimes struggled to tell us apart. Most of our friends came in sibling pairs as well, and our playdates doubled and doubled again, a chorus of childish laughter filling our days.

As adolescence crept in, we remained close, though hairline fractures began to appear in our mirrored existence. Or perhaps, I simply developed the clarity to see what had always been there. While I selected my own clothes each morning and packed my own lunches, my mother still laid out my sister's outfits and prepared her meals. Every morning, the same ritual unfolded. I laced my shoes and waited outside for my father. Eventually, curiosity would drive me back inside to discover the delay, which was always the same. My father, kneeling before my sister, tying her shoelaces with tender focus while she sat passively on the steps.

At the time, this seemed normal to me. It was just another peculiarity of family life. But years later, when my young daughter fiercely insisted on tying her shoes and selecting her clothes, the revelation struck me like lightning. There was something wrong with a teenager who couldn't, or wouldn't, tie her own shoes.

Other differences emerged. For example, my mother's expectations for me soared high. She occasionally reviewed my homework or offered suggestions, but the work remained mine alone. My sister, however, received help that often crossed the line into completion. Strangely, until recently, the inequality never even registered in my conscious thoughts.

High school continued to pull us in different directions. My sister remained quiet and withdrawn, her world consisting of one or two close girlfriends. I, on the other hand, became a social butterfly, collecting friends and boyfriends with equal enthusiasm, always in motion, always surrounded by people. We no longer wore matching outfits or shared playdates. Instead, I gravitated toward new companions while my sister retreated further into herself.

During these years, I began experimenting with marijuana, collecting detentions for skipping classes, and sneaking out after curfew. My sister never caused my parents a moment's worry, her behavior exemplary, her compliance complete. I've spent countless hours analyzing how two girls, raised in the same home by the same parents, could diverge so dramatically.

The answer, I believe, lies in how my parents sheltered my sister from even the possibility of failure. They never allowed her to stumble or to skin her knees, and consequently, she never learned to stand alone. While she never experienced homelessness or lost custody of her children, she also never discovered her own strength, never felt the fierce pride of rebuilding a life from scattered ashes.

There was one stunning exception to my sister's predictable compliance. It was a moment that shocked our family into stunned silence. She announced her intention to attend college away from home, her voice trembling but determined. It was expected that she would attend Brooklyn College, remaining within the family circle. But my sister, in a rare display of defiance, had applied to and been accepted at SUNY Albany. For once in her life, she was not just speaking, but shouting, her independence.

The night before her departure, my mother composed one of her famous poems. While most of it has faded from memory, the final line remains etched in my mind. "Bad pennies and sisters will always bounce back." I never told my sister how those words made my stomach clench. My mother subtly indicated that my sister's attempt to achieve freedom would be unsuccessful. I wish now, with an ache that feels physical, that I had gripped her shoulders and told her she would triumph, that adventure and joy awaited her in Albany. That I believed in her, even if no one else did.

My sister lasted three semesters at Albany, which required my father going up every weekend to bring her home for brief respites. Midway through her sophomore year, she transferred to Brooklyn College. We occasionally glimpsed each other on campus, and I cannot deny the selfish relief I felt having her home again. I had worried about her constantly while she was away, proving that I, too, had internalized the belief that she couldn't survive without our protection.

After my parents separated, and father relocated to Florida, my sister and I rented our first apartment together. Our parents covered the rent while we managed the utilities. By cosmic coincidence, my friend Rachel was also seeking housing, and her mother, a real estate agent, discovered a perfect two-family home on West Street in Gravesend, Brooklyn. Rachel claimed the one-bedroom downstairs while we settled into the two-bedroom upstairs. We were officially on our own, and I inherited the mantle of my sister's keeper.

My new responsibilities included chauffeuring her to and from her job at the same real estate office where I worked. It was an arrangement that chafed like an ill-fitting shoe because I worked days while she took evening shifts, thus resulting in my constant driving there back and forth. I also found myself teaching her basic household tasks that are typically learned in childhood. The irritation simmered, yet oddly, resentment never took root. I simply accepted these duties as part of the sister-package, as natural as breathing.

Nevertheless, when a friend offered me an escape route and asked me to help care for his mother in the Poconos, I seized the opportunity. I had done everything possible to teach my sister self-sufficiency, and it was now time for her to stand alone. Ironically, it was also my moment to claim independence.

When I returned to Brooklyn after my Poconos interlude, I found my sister exactly as I'd left her. She was still wearing shoes with no laces, sleeping on a bare mattress without sheets, and dropping her laundry at the local dry cleaner rather than learning to operate a washing machine. Despite these quirks, my love for her remained absolute.

I think that's why her abandonment during my darkest hours shattered something fundamental inside me. When homelessness swallowed me, my sister vanished from my life. No calls, no texts, no offers of a shower or a meal or even a kind word.

But the cruelest cut wasn't what she did but what she didn't do. She never searched for me. Not once. If our positions had been reversed, I would have combed every street, every shelter, every park bench in New York City until I found her.

Even after my parents returned to New York and I began visiting them regularly, my sister remained absent. Only after I had enrolled in college did communication slowly increase. She would occasionally read a paper I'd written, offering tentative feedback, but it was a start.

Then came the day she made her first appearance at my parents' house during one of my visits. It was a fleeting moment and nothing more substantial than a hurried hello and goodbye, but it felt monumental. My mother, overwhelmed with joy, captured the moment in a photograph. In that image, my sister looked afraid. Maybe she thought I was still the broken person who had disappeared into the city's shadows.

As she gradually accepted that I had returned not just physically but emotionally, our encounters increased. And then one day, she gave me the gift I'd wished for—I was allowed to meet my nephews. Before long, I found myself babysitting the youngest one, who was too young for daycare.

One afternoon, my sister called with an invitation for manicures. The call was casual, as if we'd never been estranged. I picked her up (she still doesn't drive), and as we merged into traffic, she turned to me, her voice soft but steady.

"I'm sure you're upset because of how I behaved while you were on the street. I was so angry with you for abandoning us that I couldn't see past that. It was wrong, and I should have done more to help you, and I'm sorry. There wasn't a day that I wasn't thinking about you and worried sick."

Those words penetrated layers of hurt and dissolved them like sugar in hot tea. Redemption, I realized, can come in unexpected packages, as do second and third chances, which are the ones I have so often needed myself.

And so, when my sister asked me to move in with my parents to help care for our father, the decision was already made in my heart before my mind could weigh the consequences. I owed this to my sister and mother, who had forgiven my many transgressions. I owed it to my father, who had loved me unconditionally through my darkest days. But most of all, I owed it to myself. This was my chance to finally prove to my family that I had returned not just in body but in spirit, and that they could depend on me when it mattered most. That I could be the daughter and sister they deserved, and perhaps had always seen in me, even when I couldn't see it in myself.

CHAPTER 19

Mother Story

"The darkest things absorb the most light."
—Sarah Elkhaldy

Traci

The walls of her parents' home seemed to close in on Maggie with each passing day. Despite the hard-won peace, living with her mother felt like navigating a minefield of unspoken resentments and raw nerves. Every glance, every sigh hung heavy in the air between them as they circled her father's sickbed—two women united by blood yet divided by decades of hurt.

There was disagreement regarding her father's care. Her mother was adamant about adhering strictly to the doctor's instructions, whereas Maggie preferred implementing comfort measures to alleviate his suffering. But it was the absence of Maggie's children that carved the deepest wound in their fragile reconciliation. Each time her father called out his grandchildren's names, Maggie felt her chest constrict with helplessness.

"They should be here," her mother would whisper, voice trembling with both grief and accusation. The words never failed to slice through Maggie. She knew it was the truth.

What her mother refused to acknowledge, however, was the cruelest truth of all—that Maggie's past mistakes had cost her not just her freedom, but the legal right to demand her children's presence. Each day that passed was another day closer to her father never seeing the children again.

Hospice offered a caregiver four hours a day, five days a week, thus allowing Maggie and her mother a little free time to do errands and attend to their own needs. One day, during this four-hour break, Maggie came into the city for a doctor's appointment of her own, and we made plans to meet up on the street for a few minutes before she headed back to Staten Island. When I saw her, Maggie was in a bad mood.

"My mom thinks I can just tell the kids to come see my dad before he dies. She knows I have no legal custody rights."

"I understand, but it's only natural that your mom is anxious about this," I said.

"True, but what can I do? Wave a magic wand?"

The bitterness in her voice was familiar—a reflection of my own past. I'd watched Maggie construct elaborate narratives that placed her mother at the center of every tragedy in her life, just as I had once done. It was easier, after all, to direct your pain outward than to let it consume you from within.

"You know what they say, right?" I asked cautiously, sensing an opening to share wisdom I'd paid dearly to learn.

"What?" Maggie said, hands on hips and fists clenched, a clear indication that she was not inclined to listen to one of my feel-good lectures.

"We're all victims of victims."

Something flashed across her face—recognition, perhaps, or the first flicker of understanding. Then, defiance hardened her features once more.

"Well, that's easy for you to say. I bet your mom told you she loved you every single day."

The air seemed to vanish from my lungs at her assumption. The truth about my mother—the story I'd been guarding like an open wound—rose to my lips, but before I could speak, fate intervened.

Maggie's phone buzzed. Her expression transformed from anger to fear as she read the message from her mother. Her father had taken a turn for the worse.

"I have to go," Maggie whispered, the color draining from her face.

The revelation I'd been avoiding—the truth about my own mother's death that might have bridged the chasm between us—would have to wait for another day. As I watched Maggie sprint down Park Avenue toward the nearest subway, her figure growing smaller against the backdrop of indifferent skyscrapers, I released a breath that felt like it had been trapped in my chest for years.

Some stories, I reminded myself, find their moment to be told.

Today was not the day for mine.

CHAPTER 20

Au Revoir, Mon Amour

"If you feel pain, you're alive.
If you feel other people's pain, you're a human being."
—Leo Tolstoy

Maggie

As I sprinted toward the subway on Park Avenue, I decided to call an Uber, instead. The subway and ferry would take two hours, and I could tell from my mother's message that the situation was not good. As the Uber sped down the highway, I wondered how it was possible that my father's health had deteriorated so quickly. It had only been six weeks since I'd moved in. I knew the situation was dire, and when I returned to my parents' house, my fears were confirmed. My father was writhing in pain, my mother by his side doing her best to soothe him. We both waited patiently for the hospice nurse to arrive.

Abu was a blessing disguised as a slight, unassuming man. I remember eyeing him doubtfully when he'd first arrived, certain his small frame would buckle under my father's weight. How wrong I was. Abu carried not just my father but all of us through those dark days, his gentle strength a lighthouse in our storm.

147

Abu's presence allowed us a few brief escapes. Some precious moments to gulp fresh air before diving back into the suffocating reality of our home. I treasured these stolen moments of normalcy.

An hour later, my father's fever spiked. In the harsh living room light, I noticed the unnatural flush on his cheeks, the glassy sheen in his eyes, mirrored in my mother's face. My stomach dropped as I reached for the COVID tests I had just administered to all three of us. I was negative. But they were both positive. Two pink lines that might as well have been a death sentence for my father. Another call to 911. Another trip to the hospital. Five days that time. Five days of pacing and praying and preparing.

When my dad returned home that Friday, the newly delivered hospital bed waited in the living room like an altar to our new reality. I greeted the ambulance outside, and as they wheeled him in, my breath caught in my throat. My dad seemed to have aged years in those five days. His frame seemed smaller to me, his skin ashen against the white sheets. He kept murmuring about the cold, though the house was stifling.

Once settled in the hospital bed, he looked around the living room. The same living room where just a mere ten days before we were sharing moments of mundane joy. My dad asked how long he'd have to stay there in that bed. I crouched beside him and looked into his eyes. Those familiar eyes, now clouded with confusion. I told him the truth. This bed was his final stop. He would never again sit at the dining room table surrounded by family. The blue sky would only ever reach him filtered through glass.

His silence stretched so long I thought he might have drifted off. When I finally asked if he was alright, his answer shattered what remained of my heart. "Why can't I just die?" What words do you say to that? I had none. I simply kissed his forehead and whispered that I was going to get him a cookie.

The following two weeks crushed us all. Dad, once so gentle and patient, became a stranger consumed by rage and frustration. He lashed out at my mother with words sharp as daggers. Even I wasn't spared his fury, something that had never happened before. I understood his anger even as it wounded me; he was raging against the dying of his light.

Abu's arrival each day became my salvation. God forgive me, but I counted the minutes until his gentle knock on the door. Those brief respites sustained me. I would escape to the backyard, marijuana smoke curling around me like a protective cloak, letting memories wash over me. I thought about Dad teaching me to ride a bike, Dad cheering me on at the spelling bee, Dad beaming with pride when my daughter reeled in her first fish by herself. And then I went back inside. The contrast was almost more than I could bear.

When Abu recommended morphine, I knew what it meant. We all did. It was the beginning of the final chapter. Traci's voice on the phone resounded in my ears. "You know what this means, right?" Those words confirmed what I couldn't bring myself to say aloud.

I paid close attention as Abu administered the first dose, his movements precise and practiced. My hands trembled as I administered the second dose to my father, watching as the lines of pain in his face slowly smoothed away. I had become the keeper of his comfort, the guardian of his passage between worlds. The weight of that responsibility pressed down on me until I could barely breathe, yet I kept moving, kept functioning, kept pretending.

When Dad could no longer help us turn him, when even gripping the side rails became impossible for him, we faced another crossroads. The options spread before us, each unpleasant. In the end, William moved in, despite his own body's rebellion. I still remember the night we decided, William holding me as I sobbed against his chest, torn between gratitude for his sacrifice and devastation at the necessity of it.

Those nights when William stayed up with Dad watching old Mike Tyson videos became sacred memories. Through my grief, a tiny flame of joy flickered. My father and William forged a bond in those midnight hours that transcended the circumstances that brought them together. Their laughter, sometimes breaking through the heavy silence of our home at 3 a.m., felt like tiny miracles.

By late February, Dad's decline accelerated. Every day took something from him. One day it was his appetite, the next his interest in music or television. The morphine doses increased, and with them, his periods of lucidity decreased. I found myself grieving him while he was still there, mourning each lost piece of him.

When Abu told us the end was near, his words merely confirmed what my heart already knew. We started calling family. Dad's sister, his cousins, his old friends. We asked them to say goodbye to a man already halfway to another shore. I watched the calendar with dread and longing, each day both too fast and unbearably slow.

February 28th dawned like any other day but quickly revealed itself as extraordinary. Dad woke up with a clarity that stole my breath. Suddenly, miraculously, he was *himself* again. His eyes, clear and focused, and his smile had returned, that same smile that had guided me through childhood. He laughed (how I'd missed that sound!) and spoke with purpose and intention.

"I love you, Maggie," he said, his hand squeezing mine with surprising strength. "These months together... I wouldn't trade them. Not even for more time." Tears flowed freely as he thanked me for my care, each word a precious gift I stored away.

To William, he spoke with the authority of a father: "Take care of my girl when I'm gone. I trust you with her." The two men shared a look of understanding that transcended words.

To my mother, he offered the most precious gift of all. The gift of forgiveness and love despite their complicated history. "I wasn't always the husband you deserved," he told her, his voice thick with emotion. "But I've always loved you."

And then came the request that made me laugh through my tears. All he wanted was one more joint. My straight-laced mother's acquiescence felt like its own small miracle. William and I exchanged conspiratorial glances as we rolled not one but four massive blunts, switching them out when Mom wasn't looking. When she narrowed her eyes suspiciously at how long the joint was lasting, we blamed it on slow-burning papers with innocent expressions that fooled no one.

Dad was gloriously, happily stoned. For a few precious hours, pain and fear retreated. We laughed together, sharing stories and memories as if we had all the time in the world. I committed every second to memory. The way the afternoon light shined in through the windows, how his fingers tapped along to the music we played, the peaceful contentment in his eyes.

It was the last good moment we would share.

The very next day, Dad woke in agony so intense it contorted his face into an unrecognizable mask. The hospice nurse's voice on the phone was gentle but direct Abu's supervisor instructed us to increase his morphine to the maximum legal dose. The medicine pulled him into a deep, dark sleep. When he surfaced briefly, he no longer asked for food. Water became his only sustenance, and even that in diminishing sips that barely wet his cracked lips.

The following days blurred together in a haze of medication schedules, whispered consultations with hospice, and brief, precious moments when Dad would emerge from the fog just long enough to smile at a visiting relative or squeeze a hand before drifting away again. The silence from a man who had filled rooms with his voice and laughter was deafening.

March 5th arrived with a heaviness I felt in my bones the moment I opened my eyes. A premonition settled over me like a shroud. I didn't know it was the last day of his life. Not consciously anyway, but something instinctual within me recognized the approaching threshold. I sent William to the liquor store before noon, something I'd never done before. The bottle felt like a lifeline in my trembling hands.

The death rattle began at midday. That terrible, unmistakable sound that once heard is never forgotten. Dad's breathing transformed into a wet, labored struggle that seemed to echo throughout the silent house. Abu assured us he wasn't suffering, that the medicine shielded him from any discomfort, but watching his body fight while his spirit was clearly ready to depart was its own unique torture.

As the sun set that night and painted the sky in watercolor shades of pink and gold, I felt the shift in the room. There was an inexplicable stillness. I lay my head gently on Dad's forehead, my tears falling onto his skin. His final breath was so soft, so subtle, I couldn't pinpoint the exact moment it happened. There was no dramatic gasp of air, no cinematic final words. It was just a gentle transition, like a river flowing seamlessly into the ocean.

The 911 call, the arrival of strangers to take away the body that had housed my father's magnificent spirit is still a blur to me. I couldn't bear to watch. After they left, I collapsed onto the empty hospital bed, my body wracked with sobs that seemed torn from the very center of my being. Grief and relief battled within me, neither winning, both true.

My dad had been ready. He'd said his goodbyes. He'd completed his journey with dignity and love. And now he was free from the prison his body had become.

And though I would carry the weight of his absence every day for the rest of my life, though I would sometimes reach for the phone to call him before remembering, though I would see his face in crowds and dreams for years to come, I, too, was free.

Free to grieve. Free to heal. Free to carry forward not just the memory of his suffering, but the legacy of his love.

Au revoir, mon amour. Until we meet again.

CHAPTER 21

Endings and Beginnings

"In the depth of winter, I finally learned that
within me there lay an invincible summer."
—**Albert Camus**

Maggie

The moment my father died, something in me died too. A pillar of my existence had crumbled, leaving me unsteady and adrift in its wake. His passing wasn't just the end of his life but also the closing of a chapter I'd not yet finished reading. I'd always believed there would be time. Time for more conversations, time for more reconciliations, time for more of his gentle wisdom. But death offers no extensions, no second chances.

The morning of his funeral dawned with a brightness that seemed to mock my grief. The sky was a vivid blue, cloudless and perfect. It was the kind of day my father would have appreciated. I resented its beauty. I stood before the mirror, eyes sunken from nights of sleepless anguish. I looked like someone older, someone broken.

But amidst this darkness came an unexpected light. My children, whom I hadn't seen in years, would be attending his funeral that morning. The last time I had seen them was in October 2021, a memory I'd replayed countless times in my head. I'm standing at the edge of a football field, Maddie's eyes a mixture of confusion and longing. But my son had been whisked away the moment the final whistle blew before I could speak to him.

Now, as we gathered at my father's open casket, my grief and joy collided. The sight of my father's casket, the polished wood containing the man who had been my foundation made my knees buckle. When it came time to say goodbye, I leaned down and pressed my lips against his cold forehead, the unfamiliar stillness of him tearing at my heart. With trembling hands, I slipped a joint into his pocket. It was a final token of our shared moments, a piece of me to accompany him on his journey.

My father had been my anchor in a life that had become unmoored. When everyone else's love came with conditions, his remained steadfast. He saw me at my worst, homeless, addicted, broken and still looked at me with eyes full of the same love he'd shown when I was a little girl full of promise. Without him, I felt exposed and vulnerable to the harsh elements of a world that had already taken so much from me.

Through my tears, I glimpsed them. My children. My daughter's face, so like mine at her age, crumpled with emotion. My son, taller than I remembered, stood rigid beside her, his expression guarded but his eyes betrayed the conflict within him. The sight of them sent a physical shock through my body, as if I'd touched a live wire. They were right there, flesh and blood extensions of my father.

Seeing them was like discovering an oasis in the desert of my grief. I drank in their images, afraid they might vanish if I blinked. My daughter had my smile, but her posture held a confidence I'd never possessed. My son had grown into his features, no longer the little boy I'd tucked into bed but a young man on the cusp of finding his own path. Time had stolen these transformations from me, and the realization pierced me anew.

In that sacred space between my father's absence and my children's presence, I felt suspended between worlds. One was ending, but there was now the possibility of another beginning. My heart, already raw from loss, expanded painfully to accommodate this new hope. The juxtaposition was almost unbearable: saying good-bye to the man who had never abandoned me while standing mere feet from the children I had left behind.

Looking at my children, I could see the threads that connected generations. We were links in a chain that stretched backward and forward through time. My father's body may have been in that casket, but his spirit lived on in their DNA, in their mannerisms, in the family stories they would one day pass down. This continuity offered a fragile comfort amid the devastation, a reminder that not everything ends, that some things merely transform.

The drive back to my mother's house after the funeral passed in a blur. My grief had a physical presence, sitting heavy on my chest, making each mile feel eternal. Yet beneath it pulsed a nervous energy. Would this tragic reunion offer a path back to my children? Could my father's final gift be the chance to rebuild what I had lost?

Hope is a dangerous thing for someone who has fallen as far as I had. Each time I'd allowed myself to hope in the past, reality had slapped me back down. But watching my children from the corner of my eye as we entered my mother's house, I couldn't help but nurture that dangerous flame.

The tension in my mother's living room was palpable. My daughter clung to me as if afraid I might disappear again, her arms wrapped around my waist, her head resting against my shoulder.

I pressed kisses to the top of her head, memorizing the feeling of holding her again.

My son, however, remained outside in the car with his father. Through the window, I could see his silhouette, determinedly facing forward. Each minute he stayed there felt like a knife twisting deeper into my heart. I understood his resistance. I'd earned it. But knowing that did nothing to ease the pain.

"Give him time," my mother whispered, her own eyes red-rimmed from crying for her husband. "He's hurting too."

When my son finally entered the house, he positioned himself as far from me as the room would allow, his gaze fixed on the floor, his shoulders rigid with tension. The physical distance between us represented years of absence, of birthdays and school events missed, of bedtime stories left untold. I wanted to cross that space, to fold him into my arms and apologize for every moment I'd missed, but I knew such a gesture would only push him further away.

Instead, I observed him from my peripheral vision, taking him in. The way his hair curled at the nape of his neck just like mine, the new freckles scattered across his nose, the adult-like way he crossed his arms over his chest. My heart ached with such ferocity that I had to remind myself to breathe. I studied every part of him, trying to imprint him on my brain in case this was the last time I saw him for a very long time.

But then I noticed a crack in his armor. Each time he thought I wasn't looking, his eyes would dart to Georgia, my sweet Chihuahua, nestled contentedly in my lap. The longing in his gaze was unmistakable. My son had always connected more easily with animals than people, finding in them an unconditional acceptance he sometimes struggled to find in humans. Including, I acknowledged with a stab of shame, his own mother.

Taking a deep breath to steady myself, I rose from my seat, Georgia cradled against my chest. Each step toward my son felt monumental, like crossing a chasm on a tightrope. I could sense my daughter watching anxiously, my mother holding her breath. When I reached him, his eyes finally met mine. He still had those beautiful eyes I'd once known better than my own. They were wary but not cold.

"Would you like to hold her?" I asked, my voice barely above a whisper, afraid that speaking too loudly might shatter this fragile moment. He nodded almost imperceptibly, and as I placed Georgia gently in his arms, the tension in his shoulders eased slightly. The smile that flickered across his face was small but genuine and it felt like I was witnessing a rare astronomical event, something precious and fleeting. My heart swelled painfully in my chest.

"We rescued her one morning during the pandemic," I said, my voice steadier now as I grasped at this tenuous connection. "Someone left her on the street in a cardboard box, soaking wet from the rain."

"How old is she?" he asked, his voice deeper than I remembered, the sound of it both familiar and strange.

"We're not sure," I replied, fighting the urge to smooth his hair as I'd done when he was small. "But the vet thinks she's somewhere around five or six. She had some health issues when we found her, but she's resilient."

"She's so cute," my son said, his finger tracing the white patch between Georgia's eyes. "Can I hold her for a little longer?"

"Absolutely," I said, my chest tight with emotion. "As long as you continue to pet her, she won't move. She's a complete attention hog." The corner of his mouth lifted at that, and I committed the image to memory. His almost smile felt like the greatest gift.

I forced myself to walk back to the other side of the room, though every maternal instinct screamed at me to stay close to him. But I knew that this moment wasn't about my needs. It was about his needs, about respecting the boundaries he'd established, about earning back his trust one tiny step at a time.

From across the room, I watched as Georgia worked her magic, my son's face softening as he stroked her fur. My daughter had moved to sit beside him, the two of them united in their admiration of the little dog who had no idea she was facilitating a family healing. In that ordinary yet extraordinary moment, I allowed myself to imagine a future where scenes like this might become commonplace again. That there might come a day when I could have my children near me, all of us finding our way back to each other.

All too soon, it was time for them to leave. The inevitable goodbye loomed like a shadow, threatening to extinguish the tiny flame of connection we'd managed to ignite. My daughter's face crumpled as she wrapped her arms around me. "I don't want to go," she whispered fiercely against my shoulder. "It's not fair."

"I know, sweetheart," I murmured, stroking her hair, trying to memorize the feel of it between my fingers. "We'll see each other again soon. I promise." It was a promise I had no authority to make, but I couldn't bear to leave her without hope.

My son approached, Georgia still cradled in his arms. The way he held her was gentle and protective and reminded me so much of how he'd been with his stuffed animals as a toddler. He transferred Georgia carefully back to me, his fingers briefly brushing against mine in the exchange.

As he turned to follow his sister toward the door, my heart seized with panic. Was that it? Would he leave without a word? But then he paused, half-turned, and said quietly, "Bye, Mom."

Mom. Not Maggie, not nothing. Mom. A simple word that most mothers hear dozens of times daily without thought, but which I hadn't heard from his lips in almost seven years. The sound of it struck me with the force of a physical blow, knocking the air from my lungs. In that single syllable lay acknowledgment, the tiniest seedling of forgiveness, perhaps even the faintest echo of love. It was everything.

I managed a nod, unable to speak past the emotion clogging my throat. And then they were gone, the door closing behind them with a finality that felt both cruel and necessary.

The moment they left, my carefully maintained composure crumbled. I stumbled into my bedroom and collapsed onto the bed, Georgia whimpering in confusion beside me. I cried for my father who was gone too soon. I cried for my children who were still present but just beyond my reach. I cried for the years lost, for the damage done, for the uncertain road ahead.

Yet even through this storm of grief, I recognized that something extraordinary had happened. On this day of profound loss, a door that had seemed permanently closed had cracked open, if only by the width of a whisper. My father was gone, but in his absence, a space had opened for my children to see me not just as the person who had left them, but perhaps as someone fighting her way back.

Grief and joy are not opposing forces as I'd once believed. They are companions that walk hand in hand through our most significant moments. The pain of losing my father would never fully leave me. It would change shape, perhaps grow less acute with time, but it would always be part of me. And now, alongside it, there existed this fragile, newborn hope of reconnection with my children.

As day faded into evening and the house grew quiet with the heavy silence that follows funerals, I found myself standing at the window. The setting sun painted the sky in shades of amber and gold, the beauty of it a reminder that even after the darkest nights, light returns. My father was gone, but he lived on in me, in my children, in the values he'd instilled and the love he'd given so freely. And my children were still here, still growing, still carrying forward our shared blood and history. In their faces, I had seen both my greatest regrets and my most profound hopes.

Gazing out that window, I made a silent vow to my father, to my children, and to myself that I would honor this day of endings and beginnings by becoming someone worthy of the second chance that had been offered. The path ahead would not be easy, but for the first time in years, it seemed possible to walk it.

Love, even in loss, never truly leaves us. It transforms, it evolves, it finds new ways to manifest. And sometimes, in our darkest hour, it returns to us in unexpected forms. A daughter's embrace, a son's tentative "Mom," a small dog bridging impossible distances. These were the gifts I carried with me from this day of grief and reunion, precious beyond measure.

CHAPTER 22

Yellow Curtains

"Darkness cannot drive out darkness; only light can do that."
—Martin Luther King, Jr.

Traci

The day Maggie's father died, it started. *Voices.* They haunted my nights, stealing my peace. Sometimes the voice belonged to my cousin Bobby, his words echoing from beyond the veil he'd crossed with morphine's cruel mercy. On darker nights, my uncle's low, rumbling tone would find me, having traveled the same shadowy path to his end. The nights became unbearable torture chambers of memory. I tossed in sweat-soaked sheets, my mind a battlefield of fragmented sleep, my body betraying me as I stumbled through days feeling as though the ground beneath me had turned to quicksand.

My mother's "visits"—once fleeting shadows at the edge of consciousness—became more frequent. Suppressed memories clawed their way upward through layers of carefully constructed denial, cracking my protective mask. I knew, with bone-deep certainty that the time had come to tell Maggie the truth about my mother's death. Until now, all she'd known was the sanitized version that my mother had died when I was in my twenties.

On the first evening of Jewish Passover—April 5, 2023—my carefully constructed walls finally crumbled. Though raised Christian, the story of Passover had been etched into my heart since childhood, one of the first sacred tales I'd absorbed in Sunday school, still wide-eyed and believing in miracles.

Passover. Moses leading his people from the chains of Egyptian slavery. The mysterious, breathtaking parting of the Red Sea— waters parting, standing like glass walls while the Israelites walked to freedom. And now, after decades of carrying this burden, I too stood at the edge of my own Red Sea, trembling at the prospect of freedom.

That night, she came and refused to leave. I jolted awake, heart thundering, as I *felt* another presence in my bedroom. I sat upright, eyes straining through darkness that revealed nothing. I was alone. Joel was away on business. Convinced I was trapped in some half-dream state, I forced myself to lie back down.

And then, I heard her voice.

"Are you listening, Suzie?"

My mother used the nickname she'd given me when I was a child. My name had been a battlefield in our family from the beginning, a skirmish in the larger war. My father had insisted on Traci, honoring a fallen brother-in-arms from WW2. My mother had fought for Barry Jo with a passion that eventually withered after my brother's birth. My grandfather had settled on Sam, my brother called me Sissy, and my mother—oh, my mother—had called me Suzie, as if baptizing me anew with each utterance.

Fully awake now, my heart pounded, I feared the fragile threads of my sanity were finally unraveling. Surely this was just a nightmare, a cruel trick of an exhausted mind. Yet it felt so real. Too real. The room around me dissolved, and suddenly I was transported backward through time and space to another bed, another year, another house.

◆ ◆ ◆

The phone's shrill cry tore through the silence at 6:00 a.m. on June 26, 1978. I jerked awake, disoriented in the unfamiliar bedroom of my future in-laws' home, where Joel and I were staying for the summer before our August wedding. Even before my fingers touched the receiver, I *knew*. The knowledge lived not in my mind but in my body like a primal, animal certainty. The hair on my arms stood rigid at attention, electricity flooding my system with fight-or-flight chemicals. I wanted to run, but there was no escape.

"Hello?" My voice emerged thin and tremulous, the question mark punctuating the end of my greeting.

"Rug is dead." My brother's voice, flat, hollowed, unrecognizable. The nickname he'd given our mother seemed obscene now, a remnant from a world that no longer existed. He'd called her that because her short hair perched atop her head like a rug.

"Rug is dead," Jeff repeated, his voice cracking with effort—partly to convince himself the impossible words had truly left his lips, partly to ensure I'd heard the unthinkable truth.

"I will be on the next plane home," I whispered. The phone slipped from my nerveless fingers, clattering against the nightstand as a scream rose from the deepest part of me. It was the sound of something vital being ripped away, leaving a wound that would never fully heal.

When we entered Washington National airport, my eyes frantically searched the sea of faces until locking onto my brother and father. The sight of them made the nightmare real in a way nothing else had. During the silent car ride to my grandmother's house, my father finally spoke, his voice devoid of life, and told us what little he knew. Jeff sat beside him in the front seat, staring sightlessly through the windshield, as if hoping to find an alternate reality beyond the glass.

When my father saw my mother's wedding rings placed with care on the nightstand, he knew something was wrong. Entering our den, the acrid smell of exhaust fumes assaulted him.

"I already knew where she was," he confessed, voice breaking. "I just couldn't bring myself to look inside the car yet." Instead, he threw open the garage door, desperate to let clean air rush in, as if it might somehow undo what had been done. Only then did he force himself to approach the car.

With trembling hands, my father lifted my mother's body from the driver's seat. Her skin—already cold—felt like a stranger's beneath his touch. He carried her inside and laid her gently on the living room couch as if she might still wake from a deep sleep. Despite the oppressive June heat, he covered her with her favorite blanket, tucking it tenderly around her shoulders one final time.

Then he descended the stairs to my brother's basement bedroom. Jeff was showering in the spiral-shaped stall that needed no door. My father poked his head in and around the first curve. Before Jeff could process the apparition of his father's face appearing beneath the same running water, our father spoke the words that would divide Jeff's life into before and after.

"Your mom is dead."

Jeff stepped out, water still cascading behind him. His face contorted, his chin making a terrible, unnatural shift from left to right as if the foundations of his features were crumbling. Grabbing a towel, his skin still dripping, he ascended to the kitchen to call me—his older sister—the one who was supposed to know what to do.

Three hours later, we stood in my grandmother's kitchen. She knew something had happened the moment we appeared at her door unannounced. Still wrapped in her faded floral bathrobe, coffee steaming in her favorite mug, and her newspaper spread before her—the ordinary morning that was about to be shattered.

I couldn't bear to look at her. Instead, I fixed my gaze everywhere else—the ancient stove with its temperamental burners, the yellow Formica counters, the faded curtains that had framed countless family gatherings. I memorized the delicate pattern of small flowers on the wallpaper. I stared through the window at a world that continued to exist, despite what had happened.

I couldn't bear to look at her. Instead, I looked at the old stove, at the yellow Formica counters, and the curtains. I studied the pattern of small flowers on the wallpaper. I stared out the window. I looked beyond, above, and around but not at her.

She looked at us, stood up, and stumbled backward, clutching her chest. My father didn't prolong her growing alarm.

"Mary, sit down please."

Ignoring his suggestion and her chair, she continued backing away from us as if she could avoid whatever was coming next. My father put his arms around her.

"I'm so sorry, but Jean is dead."

My grandmother's face twisted into unnatural opposing directions. She steadied herself and asked an utterly simplistic question. "How can that be? She is only forty-nine years old."

Again, in consideration of her rising anxiety, my father did not delay his explanation. "I'm so sorry, Mary, but she killed herself last night."

My grandmother fell to the ground and, pounding the kitchen floor with her clenched fists, started screaming, "Not my Jean! Not my Jean!" The ancient, animal sound of a mother losing her child echoed off the walls, a sound never meant to be heard in this world.

◆ ◆ ◆

I was awakened by my own screams, with the bedsheets ensnaring my limbs like restraints. I was back in my apartment, my nightgown soaked with cold sweat. There was no telephone in my bedroom. There hadn't been one since that fateful night when my brother called. Early morning phone calls, and especially ones in the middle of the night, have a certain tone to them, alerting the senses that bad news is arriving.

I fell back to sleep. I heard my mother's voice for the second time that night. "I want to tell you a story, and please let me finish before you ask any questions."

"I only have one question, Mom," I whispered into the darkness. "*Why?*" The word emerged broken, ragged with decades of pain.

"Just listen," she urged, her voice achingly familiar. "Your brother and I were watching a basketball game. It was getting late, so I turned off the TV and told him to go to bed because the next day would be a long one. He thought I meant work, but, of course, I wasn't referring to his summer job. My mind was made up. I intended to do it that night. I'd wanted to spare your father and brother the trauma of finding my body, but my earlier plan had failed."

I remembered the story with sickening clarity. A week before her death, my mother had decided to quit taking Valium cold turkey, voluntarily checking herself into the hospital. In 1978, doctors didn't understand that Valium addiction required a slow, weaning process. They had allowed her to try.

One night, after the nurse had completed her final rounds, my mother had attempted to force the window open, intending to plunge to the pavement below. By some cruel twist of fate— or mercy, depending on one's perspective—the nurse heard the struggle and summoned security.

I knew I was asleep and willed myself, without success, to wake up. My mother continued her story. "That's when I made the decision. The next morning, I checked myself out. That afternoon I went to the library and read about the effects of carbon monoxide poisoning. It sounded like a peaceful way to die. I'd lived so long as an addict and believed whatever came next would be better."

"Were you afraid?" I asked, my voice childlike.

"Not exactly, but I did say a prayer."

I jerked awake a second time, my body drenched in sweat despite the warm room. Sleep had abandoned me completely now. Shaken to my core, I sat in the darkness, replaying what I imagined were my mother's final moments, alone in our family car, sealed in our garage.

She wouldn't have felt pain. This much I knew. The carbon monoxide would have lulled her gently, stealing her awareness before she realized death had arrived. Yet I wondered if, in those final moments of clarity, she'd experienced regret. Had she reached for the door handle? Had she thought of me, of Jeff, of Dad?

But no. My mother had nerves of steel and a determination that bordered on the terrifying. Once she committed to a course of action, nothing on earth could dissuade her. If she'd noticed the first subtle signs of the poison's effect—the dizziness, the heaviness—she would have steeled herself, clenched her fists against any instinctive panic, and surrendered to her choice with the same fierce resolve that had defined her life.

I wondered what prayer my mother, an atheist, might have said that night. And then I remembered the postcard she'd kept taped to her mirror in the upper left-hand corner.

God, grant me the serenity to accept the things
I cannot change, the courage to change the things I can,
and the wisdom to know the difference.

CHAPTER 23

Awakening

"A smooth sea never made a skilled sailor."
—Franklin Delano Roosevelt

Maggie

Traci finally told me about her mother's suicide. As she spoke, I stood paralyzed, listening to what she said yet unable to grasp the enormity of her words. Tears stung my eyes as my own "mother" memories resurfaced, bubbling up from places I'd tried desperately to seal shut.

◆ ● ◆

I was a typical teenager, rebellious and irresponsible, though my report cards never showed it. I stumbled through my high school years, leaving a trail of mistakes in my wake that seemed innocuous at the time but would haunt me for decades. I cut classes, snuck out of the house, and crafted elaborate lies about my whereabouts, each one easier than the last.

My mother and I existed in perpetual conflict, two storms colliding. Yet beneath the thunder of our arguments burned my undeniable adoration for her. She is brilliant in ways that still leave me in awe. She breathes Shakespeare as naturally as air, crafts poems that can make strangers weep, and possesses an instinctive, almost magical taste in everything from the delicate arrangement of throw pillows to the perfect pair of sneakers.

While I've always adored my father with a quiet, steady love, it's my mother who dominates the landscape of my childhood memories. Some shine with unexpected warmth, like the afternoon she transformed our living room into an impromptu picnic ground, her smile genuine and unburdened as my sister and I sprawled across the floor. When I knocked over my soda, watching in horror as it seeped into the pristine carpet, she just laughed and helped me blot it dry. Or the Saturday morning I woke to find three boxes of Jordan sneakers waiting for me, her eyes gleaming with satisfaction at my speechless joy. But these golden moments are islands in a sea of darker memories. Those are the ones that carved me into the person I am today.

In third grade, I lost the spelling bee in the final round on the word "embarrassed." My mother had come to watch, her presence both a comfort and a source of terror. When we met afterward, her face revealed neither consolation nor pride that I'd made it so far. Instead, her words sliced through me. "Really, Maggie? You lose on the word *embarrassed*? That must have been *embarrassing* for you." The memory still makes my stomach clench. I can still feel the burning shame that spread through my eight-year-old body, the desperate wish to disappear as other parents hugged their children just feet away. Now I understand that so many of my later deceptions were born at that moment. Desperate attempts to never again feel the particular agony of disappointing her.

Through the years, similar moments accumulated like bruises on young children playing tag. Nights when my sleep would shatter to the sound of her voice, yanking me into consciousness just to berate me for some transgression hours old. Though physically slight, never once striking me, her words could flatten me more effectively than any blow. Her favorite punishment was public humiliation. She made sure my friends witnessed my disgrace. She also enjoyed the destruction of things I cherished. I learned to navigate my days around her moods, my existence a continuous effort to avoid her disapproval.

The day my mother moved out of our home when I was nineteen, euphoria flooded through me like sunlight. *Freedom!* Just my sister, father, and me in a house suddenly spacious with possibility! But my joy evaporated with unsettling speed, leaving behind a puzzling emptiness.

Something shifted inside me when she left. Through the lens of distance, I began to see her differently. Not just as the tyrannical guardian of my behavior, but as a woman who had endured an unhappy marriage for years, sacrificing her own peace for some twisted definition of family. I recognized the quiet desperation that had fueled her anger, and found myself reluctantly impressed by her courage to finally sever those chains.

To my astonishment, our visits at her new place unfolded without the familiar soundtrack of shouting or criticism. We existed in a fragile but precious peace. When her companion and dearest friend received a glioma diagnosis, I witnessed a side of my mother I'd never seen before. I watched her fierce loyalty and tenderness as she stood unwavering through his deterioration, holding his hand until his final breath. A new respect bloomed in me, reluctant but undeniable.

After she relocated to Florida, another metamorphosis occurred in our relationship. Our daily phone calls became rituals I looked forward to rather than dreaded. I found myself eager to share stories of my children, and she listened with a presence that had always eluded her before. We had finally reached a place of mutual respect, the battleground of our past grown over with tentative new growth. And then I had that fateful root canal, and watched helplessly as opioids consumed everything I'd built.

Looking back now, with eyes sharpened by experience, my perspective on my mother has transformed yet again. Yes, she yelled with a fury that made the walls seem to vibrate. But the worst tangible thing she ever did was destroy my beloved stuffed clown, Mr. George, his dismembered limbs scattered across my bedroom floor like casualties of her rage. Now, I understand how comparatively fortunate I was. She never hit me. Ever. Many of my friends, Traci included, bore the physical evidence of discipline. Angry welts from tree switches, the distinctive pattern of a leather belt impressed upon tender skin. The neighborhood boys fared worse, sporting black eyes and split lips with disturbing regularity. Those were days when "spare the rod and spoil the child" wasn't just a saying but a parenting philosophy, passed through the neighborhood like children playing soccer.

There was one other incident before Mr. George's execution that stuck with me, and that was the destruction of my Hubert Davis jersey. We'd hunted for it for years, long before the internet made any desire instantly available. Davis, now the head coach of North Carolina's men's basketball team, had always represented to me a rare combination of unshakable character and raw determination.

One afternoon after school, I found the jersey sliced down the middle, the fabric gaping open like a wound. Though devastated at the time, I must now admit my mother had justification. At thirteen, I'd crossed a boundary that couldn't be ignored.

I'd started babysitting for our neighbor Cindy, whose hand-crafted jewelry made her a minor celebrity in our community. One evening, noticing an open cabinet in her living room bookshelf, I discovered something far more valuable than her artistic creations. Inside were bags of marijuana and stacks of money bound in rubber bands. Clearly, Cindy's entrepreneurial spirit extended beyond jewelry design.

At the time, I wasn't particularly shocked. My father smoked pot regularly, a fact I discovered when I innocently asked him about his "magic grass" and watched panic flash across his face as he snatched it away. Another memory surfaced: the afternoon at the local pool hall when older kids lit a joint, and I naively asked, "Who's wearing Brut?" Their laughter still echoes in my mind. It was the moment when my father's familiar scent suddenly made terrible sense.

During my next babysitting job for Cindy, temptation overwhelmed my better judgment. With so many bags of marijuana in her possession, surely she wouldn't miss a small amount? Eventually, inevitably, she noticed. Unable to admit her illicit business, she accused me of stealing two hundred dollars. It was a lie, but one I couldn't refute without revealing her secret. The consequences cascaded. My babysitting job vanished, my precious jersey was destroyed, and most devastating of all, I watched something vital crumble in my mother's eyes when she looked at me. Trust, once broken, leaves jagged edges that never quite fit together again.

I don't think I ever fully trusted myself after that day, either. We can spin elaborate deceptions for the world, but our own hearts know the unvarnished truth.

◆ ◆ ◆

Until the day Traci shared her "mother story" with me, the destruction of Mr. George and my jersey had loomed in my mind as unforgivable betrayals. But as she spoke, her voice sometimes dropping to a whisper so soft I had to lean in to hear, the truth crashed over me with devastating clarity. How trivial my grievances suddenly seemed, how shallow my understanding of suffering.

Standing on that corner, listening to Traci's story, an unfamiliar anger surged through me. The anger was not at my mother this time, but at myself. My head throbbed with self-recrimination, my fingernails cutting half-moons into my palms as my hands involuntarily clenched into fists. Then, like a second wave, came the guilt, which was crushing and absolute. My mother was *alive*. Despite everything, my lies, my addiction, and my failures she hadn't abandoned me. She was still there, somehow still believing in the possibility of my redemption when I'd given up on myself long ago.

I had placed Traci on a pedestal, and thought the sun rose and set with her. I was convinced her life must have unfolded in picture-perfect scenes. How else could she have become the woman standing before me? In my mind, she inhabited a world untouched by the shadows that had followed me. The revelation that she had navigated her own darkness, her own unspeakable pain, shattered my assumptions and forged an unexpected bond between us.

As we exchanged our stories, raw and unvarnished, something shifted inside me. The anger I'd carried for so long, that familiar weight I'd almost grown comfortable with, began to loosen its grip. In its place bloomed an overwhelming tenderness for Traci, a recognition so profound it left me breathless. *Kindred spirit.* The words surfaced in my mind with absolute certainty.

The parallels in our histories were undeniable, yet we had arrived at such different destinations. She stood surrounded by a family she'd built with love and intention, while I had failed spectacularly at both marriage and motherhood, hundreds of miles separating me from children who were growing up without me. This discrepancy haunted me. Why had she flourished while I had faltered? What inner strength had she discovered that continued to elude me?

Through our conversations in the days that followed, a realization began to take shape. I had been clutching my anger toward my mother like a shield, using it to deflect responsibility for my own choices. It was time, long past time, to let it go.

Traci's story forced me to confront the painful reality of my relationship with my own daughter. I barely recognized what it meant to be a present mother anymore. I had become her friend rather than her parent, offering the unconditional love I'd always craved from my own mother but withholding the boundaries and guidance of the tough love she desperately needed. Now that she was navigating the treacherous waters of adolescence, I could finally understand some of my mother's choices with painful clarity. I prayed for another chance to be the mother my children deserved, though the fear that I had irreparably lost my son haunted my sleepless nights.

That day, as Traci's words settled into my soul, something fundamental shifted. For the first time, I stopped pointing accusatory fingers at my mother, at Danny, at my mother-in-law, at the cruel indifference of the world. Instead, I turned that finger inward, acknowledging with terrifying clarity that I alone had authored my current circumstances.

That moment of brutal self-honesty, as painful as it was, marked the beginning of my awakening.

CHAPTER 24

JAT

"I can't change the direction of the wind,
but I can adjust my sails."
—Jimmy Dean

Traci

After Maggie's father was buried, miracles started to happen. First, out of the blue, Brooklyn College recalculated Maggie's credits and informed her she only needed six more courses to graduate. The news had brought tears to Maggie's eyes. And to mine.

Second, against all odds, *Unsheltered Love* won the Eric Hoffer grand prize. I remember the exact moment I found out, the surge of disbelief washing over me. A notice popped up in my email announcing that the winner had been selected. It was a generic message sent to the thousands of authors and publishers who had entered a title, so I didn't think much of it at the time. Nevertheless, out of curiosity, I decided to see who the winner was. When my eyes focused on *Unsheltered Love*, the room seemed to tilt beneath me. I once again thought I might be delusional—joy and vindication colliding in my chest.

The third and most important miracle for me personally was when my cousin Torey sent me a few things she'd found in her recently-deceased mother's bible. One of them was a letter I'd written to my mother when I was nineteen. It sat on my dresser for months, its edges yellowing, taunting me with ghosts I wasn't ready to face. Each morning I would brush my fingertips across it, feeling the weight of unspoken words heavier than the paper itself.

One summer weekend, I went upstate to our house on the lake, my sanctuary from the noise of New York City, and more importantly, my own thoughts. I took the letter with me, tucked into my jacket pocket, and finally found the courage to read it. My hands trembled so much I could barely unfold the fragile paper.

◆ ◆ ◆

March 24, 1975
Dear Mom,

I don't know how to say what I want to because I never seem to be good with words when it comes to saying something from my heart. First, I want to say that I'm sorry for the way I acted during spring break. I know nothing I say is going to take away the hurt or heal the scars, but I really want you to know that I love you so much and will always appreciate everything you've done for me. I know you've sacrificed your whole life for me, and I'm appalled at myself for my selfish actions.

Thank you so much for the gifts—that was so sweet of you. I can't believe how good you are to me. I hope you understand that I have my faults, and I am really trying to correct them, but it seems to be very hard to do. Please understand and give me just a little more time to grow up. It's taking a long time and the road seems to be very long and hard to travel, but I'm trying. I would die if it would give you the chance to live. Please help me grow and learn. I have so much left to learn!

Love, Traci

◆ ◆ ◆

I dropped the letter as if it had scaled my fingertips and stared at the third line from the bottom. *I would die if it would give you the chance to live.* A cold, primal dread crawled up my spine. Did I somehow know my mother's death was imminent? She was only forty-six at the time.

My mother's face, a long-suppressed memory, came into focus, cutting through decades of deliberate forgetting. Her smile—always tinged with melancholy—her eyes that seemed to carry oceans of unspoken sorrows. I allowed myself to remember the last time I'd spoken to her, on the evening of June 25, 1978, only hours before she drew her last carbon monoxide breath. The memory clawed its way from the depths where I'd buried it, every detail suddenly vivid and excruciating.

"Please remember one thing—whatever happens, I love you."

It was the first and last time she spoke those three words to me. Now they echoed across the years, each syllable a hammer striking the same broken bell.

The sun was about to set over the lake, painting the water in shades of crimson and gold. I was alone on the dock, waves created from passing boats breaking at my feet. A lone seagull flew overhead in search of its dinner, its cry piercing the evening quiet. I wondered how a seagull, an omnipresent sight at the ocean, had found its way to fresh water, lost and displaced, just as I had been for so long.

A few minutes later it reappeared, a freshly caught fish in its claws, struggling and glistening in the dying light. I watched the fish's futile thrashing slow and then cease, reminding me that even in paradise sacrifices must be made, and sometimes, there is no escape. Not for that fish. Not for Maggie. Not for me.

I'd run as fast and as far as I could for one lifetime, each step fueled by grief I refused to name, each new achievement a flimsy shelter against the storm I couldn't face. There was no place for me to go except within—into the very darkness I had spent decades fleeing.

That was the beginning of my inward journey. It was almost as if my eyeballs literally rotated in their sockets, turning away from the distractions of the external world to finally witness the wreckage within. After that day, my focus remained inward, excavating layers of pain, regret, and unprocessed grief that had accumulated like sediment over a lifetime.

I had become the captain of the proverbial ship, albeit with sails torn and frayed from years of emotional storms, bow full of leaks from the weight of memories I'd tried to drown. But it was still afloat on the open seas with me seated by the rudder.

CHAPTER 25

The Road to Freedom

"The fiat of the Almighty, 'Let there be light,'
has not yet spent its force."
—Frederick Douglass

Maggie

The fall of 2023 was a challenging time. William's health hung by a thread so fragile I couldn't leave him alone for even a moment. I'd hire babysitters anytime I had to leave the house, constantly checking my phone, terrified of what news might come.

And then, on a day that started like any other, flames devoured our entire world.

William and I were asleep in the apartment when we were awoken by our neighbor's screams. "The house is on fire!!" I grabbed Georgia and frantically tried to get William up and out of the house. In the middle of the chaos, I realized I could not find my cat, Tyson. With no time to waste, I had no choice but to run out of the house, one slipper on, the heat of the flames searing my face.

Everything we owned was gone. Everything we'd scraped together after years of having nothing vanished in that blaze.

Our furniture, clothes, the pots and pans, the washing machine I'd been so proud to own, the TV that had given us moments of escape, and my computer, which was a lifeline to education and a future. All turned to dust. And we never saw Tyson again.

Our agency relocated us to another apartment in the same neighborhood. Six flights of stairs separated us from the outside world, six treacherous flights that William faced with quivering legs. Each step was a battle against his failing body, each landing a brief respite where he'd lean against the wall, eyes closed, gathering his courage for the next flight. I'd watch him, my heart splintering, torn between admiration for his determination and despair at his suffering.

Amidst the turmoil and loss, I registered for two Monday classes for the spring semester and secured a babysitter for the day. In those precious hours away, memories would ambush me without warning. When I'd lived on the street, which seemed both a lifetime ago and just yesterday, I would lose myself in desperate daydreams about all I'd lost. My children's faces would swim before me, so clear I could almost touch them. Two other treasures haunted my dreams: a key, a simple piece of metal that meant safety, dignity, belonging and a dog, whose unconditional love would remind me I was still human, still worthy.

I'd watch people hurry past, their lives so normal, so secure, and envy would come. I'd yearned with every fiber of my being to be one of them again. But the brutal truth I'd witnessed on the streets was that almost no one makes it back. The current of homelessness pulls you under and rarely releases its grip. The lucky ones like me are so few, I could count them on one hand with fingers to spare.

Now, the keys to my apartment lay on my dresser. Real keys to a real home. Georgia, the light of my life, was never far from my side. Before the fire, Tyson would perch regally atop the refrigerator, yellow eyes narrowed as he watched me study, his presence a comfort I never knew I needed until it was gone.

This miracle, an improbable second chance, doesn't happen to people like me. Most of those I'd met on the streets never escaped. They shuffled between shelters, group homes, and dingy, single-room occupancies, trapped in a purgatory between homelessness and home. They didn't get apartments with air fryers and washing machines and air conditioning that hummed soothingly on hot summer nights.

This was exactly what I'd dreamed of through endless nights of homelessness, with dirt embedded so deeply under my fingernails it seemed permanent, and a hollowness in my stomach that no amount of donated food could fill. I had everything I'd pictured in my head on those never ending nights.

So why did misery still cling to me like a second skin?

At first, I dismissed it as temporary. It was just a bad day, a rough week, a difficult couple of months. But as the darkness persisted, suffocating and relentless, and I finally faced the truth: something fundamental was broken, and that something was inside me.

Self-loathing washed over me in waves. How dare I be ungrateful? I had walls to protect me, a roof that didn't leak, warmth when others froze on sidewalks. My daughter's voice, that beautiful voice I'd thought I'd never hear again, now filled my ears every day. My mother, sister, and nephews had welcomed me back into the family I'd once abandoned. A man loved me despite knowing every ugly detail of my past. I was back in college! What right did I have to this crushing unhappiness?

The question echoed unanswered in my mind as Monday became my lifeline. It was the one day when I could escape, if only briefly. On campus, I dissolved into the sea of students, anonymous and blessedly ordinary. For those few precious hours, I could pretend I was just like them. But the illusion always shattered the moment class ended.

Homelessness had rewired something fundamental in me, had altered my DNA in ways I was only beginning to understand. The further I moved from that life, the more its shadow lengthened behind me. The weight of my second chance pressed down on my chest like a stone. What if I wasted it? What if I failed again? The possibility paralyzed me.

Each morning, I'd wake with a knot of anxiety already tightening in my stomach. Would we eat today? Would this be the day William's seizures finally took him from me? Would this be the day I finally surrendered to the exhaustion that had seeped into my bones?

During one visit to my mother's, she asked how things were going, her eyes landing on me with concern. Something inside me cracked open, and tears I didn't know I'd been holding back flooded out in a torrent that left me gasping. Between sobs that tore at my throat, I confessed how overwhelmed I felt, constantly on duty, never allowed a moment to just *be*. I felt crushed by an invisible debt. A penance for all my past mistakes that demanded I be available to everyone who needed me, regardless of what it cost me.

The truth I could hardly admit, even to myself, was that resentment toward William had begun to fester in my heart. The constant care, the endless vigilance, the cleaning and soothing and worrying was consuming the person I'd hoped to become. I'm still ashamed to write these words, but I wanted more than a life defined by caregiving. I craved space to breathe, to dream, to just exist without someone depending on my every move.

Sleep became a luxury I could no longer afford. Two to four hours a night was all I managed, jolting awake to check his breathing, clean up after accidents, or stand guard when the telltale signs of an impending seizure appeared. Hospital corridors and doctors' waiting rooms became more familiar than my own living room. Despite five different anti-seizure medications with doses that kept climbing, the seizures continued their relentless assault on his body and his mind.

One night before Thanksgiving we were watching TV in bed on an otherwise uneventful day. William was mid-sentence when his voice simply stopped, as if someone had cut a string. When I turned to him, the sight froze my blood. His eyes, the eyes that had once looked at me with such love, were vacant, dark pools staring into nothingness. His body had gone rigid and I was frozen in the moment.

I snapped out of it and shook him until I felt his muscles finally release their grip. But when he looked at me, there was no recognition in his gaze. There was only confusion and growing fear. For the first time since I'd known him, I was afraid of the man I loved. He stared wildly around the room, pushing me away when I tried to explain, his panic feeding my own until I thought I might shatter from it. Only when I thrust Georgia into his line of sight did something flicker and soften in his expression.

Hours later, just as relief had begun to loosen the knot in my chest, a full seizure ripped through him with such violence that we both crashed to the floor. By some miracle, I managed to wedge a pillow between his head and the furniture before it could split his skull open. When consciousness finally returned to him, he mumbled about a headache that pulsed "inside and out." I gave him Tylenol, watching as sleep soothed him while I remained painfully, exhaustingly awake.

With sleep impossible, I reached for *The Power of Now* by Eckhart Tolle. The story of a beggar unknowingly sitting on a box of gold for years struck me with bitter irony. That night, I felt scraped clean of anything resembling gold or worth. Yet something in Tolle's words pierced through my exhaustion. I'd been searching for validation, security, and love everywhere except within myself. The Buddha taught that enlightenment is the end of suffering. I desperately needed that enlightenment. What remains when suffering ends? Peace. A word so foreign to me it might as well have been in another language.

I fell asleep with the book on my chest, one ear strained for sounds of distress, one eye half-open against the darkness. Between the demands of school and William's care, meaningful employment had become an impossible dream. Though our rent was subsidized, food stamps stretched only so far. Hunger became our unwelcome companion, a familiar gnawing that I tried to ignore.

What I needed was remote work. Something to do from home while watching over William. I'd already lost my personal assistant position twice: first to care for my dying father, then again for William. My dream, a small, fragile thing I hardly dared acknowledge, was an entry-level job at a publishing house. Reading, writing, editing. These were skills I possessed. My work with Unsheltered Love had even given me publishing experience. But dreams and reality rarely aligned in my world, and this one seemed particularly far-fetched.

Meanwhile, William's seizures multiplied like cancer cells. I fought daily battles with doctors, insurance companies, and hospital administrators, all while watching his mind deteriorate before my eyes.

The changes were subtle at first. So subtle I could almost pretend they weren't happening. He'd repeat stories he'd told just minutes before, his eyes bright with enthusiasm as if sharing them for the first time. On the subway, confusion would cloud his face, familiar stations suddenly foreign territory. William, who once knew every shortcut and back alley in Manhattan like they were extensions of his own body, would look around with the lost expression of a tourist. I made jokes to ease the tension, blaming "the scrambles" in his brain, suggesting he cut back on weed and alcohol, anything to avoid facing the terrifying truth.

By November, we could no longer hide from reality. The seizures came with brutal frequency, each one more severe, each one stealing another piece of him. His body bore the evidence. Stitched wounds from falls, a tongue partly bitten in half during a violent episode. Uncertainty had become his constant companion, leaving him afraid to venture outside alone.

His short-term memory vanished. We'd spend an hour at the supermarket carefully selecting ingredients for dinner, and on the walk home, he'd turn to me with innocent curiosity and ask, "So what do you want to get for dinner?"

Then, a miracle appeared. Riding the subway home one night, my eyes caught on a sign advertising FreedomCare, a program working with Medicaid to pay friends or family members for providing in-home care to eligible patients. My pulse quickened as I read, hope fluttering dangerously in my chest for the first time in months.

I called the number, starting the qualification process with desperate optimism. After submitting forms granting access to William's medical records, we scheduled an in-person interview.

When the nurse arrived at our apartment, William put on a heartbreaking performance. Part of him still rebelled against his illness, and he struggled to appear normal, to be the man he used to be. But his unsteady gait betrayed him, as did the circular conversations where he'd forget what he'd said moments before. As she prepared to leave, the nurse's words, "he qualifies for the program", flooded me with relief. One final hurdle remained: confirmation from their doctor.

That appointment came a week later. The doctor's examination was thorough, his review of William's medical history meticulous. When he finally looked up and agreed that William qualified for FreedomCare, tears sprang to my eyes, too sudden to hide.

Next came my approval as his caregiver, a FreedomPro in the program's terminology. The requirements seemed slightly overwhelming. Online orientation classes, twenty hours of hands-on training, medical forms, vaccination records, identification verification. But for the first time in years, paperwork and requirements didn't feel like obstacles. They felt like stepping stones to salvation.

The duties listed—helping with personal care, meal preparation, medication management, appointment accompaniment, housework, and grocery shopping—were things I already did every day. The difference was staggering though. Now these acts of love would also help us survive.

Two weeks later, I began my online classes with single-minded determination. After completing forty hours, I moved on to in-person training at a Bronx assisted-living facility, absorbing everything I could, failure not an option.

On December 6, 2023 I officially became a FreedomPro and worked my first paid shift. The significance wasn't lost on William. Through the fog of his illness, I saw a spark of the old pride in his eyes. One of the cruelest aspects of his condition had been watching him struggle with feelings of uselessness. Now, somehow, his illness had become our lifeline, and the irony of that gave him a measure of peace I hadn't seen in months.

The financial impact was immediate and profound. The constant, grinding anxiety of poverty, of wondering how we'd eat, how we'd survive another day had been physically aging me, strands of gray appearing in my hair overnight. Now, I had a steady income. But the greatest gift wasn't financial for me. It was freedom. Freedom from constant panic. Freedom to breathe. Freedom to believe, however cautiously, that tomorrow might be better than today.

I am beyond grateful. Some words are too small to contain the overwhelming tide of emotion that rises when I think about how far we've come. In the midst of our darkest winter, we found, improbably, impossibly, our invincible summer.

CHAPTER 26

The Secret

*"Everything is energy and that's all there is to it.
Match the frequency of the reality you want and you cannot help
but get that reality. This is not philosophy. This is physics."*
—**Darryl Anka**

Traci

I remember the exact day it happened—unbelievably, at the same moment—to both of us. The memory is etched in my mind like a scar. But I never minded my scars—emotional or physical. Scars don't form on the dead. Those scars meant I'd survived.

It was Maggie's spring break from school, and we'd made plans to meet up for lunch in the city. A few weeks earlier, Maggie and William had been moved to a third apartment. The location was not ideal—far from it. However, the building had a live-in superintendent, who was willing, if not anxious, to stay with William in exchange for $40 a day. Another compromise in Maggie's increasingly complicated life.

After a pleasant lunch filled with laughter, Maggie and I stood on the street corner. The spring sunshine blessed our faces, though it couldn't quite penetrate the chill that had settled in our hearts years ago. As was often the case, the subject of our discussion drifted to our mothers—always our mothers. That magnetic pull of unresolved pain that always seemed to draw us back.

How we had wallowed in our victim mentality. The comfort of that familiar narrative had wrapped around us like a blanket for so long that we couldn't imagine life without it. However, when I told Maggie about my mother's death, something shifted in her eyes. In that raw moment of my vulnerability, she realized the things her mother had done were not the unforgivable crimes she'd built them up to be. And, at the same moment, like lightning striking us both, I realized that despite my mother's devastating choice to end her own life, she had never once, in any way, shape, or form, belittled me. Unlike Maggie, my mother had never told me I was unworthy, or made me feel inadequate. She had carried her own unbearable darkness, but she had never projected it onto me.

Those realizations were just the beginning—the first domino in a cascade of truth. We also, and again at the same heart-stopping moment, realized that being in a victim mentality only attracted more things to feel victimized about. Our pain had been calling to more pain, our wounds attracting fresh injuries. As the quote above reveals, our vibrations attract similar vibrations. We had been broadcasting our suffering to the universe, and the universe had faithfully answered.

My favorite subject in school was physics, so it made sense to me on an intellectual level. I'm not sure how or why Maggie received the same message at the identical moment. Perhaps it was my own realization that traveled to her brain like electricity jumping between wires, or perhaps it was the other way around. Or perhaps our souls had synchronized in that sunlit moment of truth. Regardless, we both realized with stunning clarity that—whether it was "warranted" or not—being in a victim mentality only ensured the continuation of feeling victimized. We had been our own jailers.

However, that is not the secret referred to in the subtitle of this book. That revelation hit even closer to home, cutting to the very foundation of our identities. While we both had endless complaints about our mothers—cataloged and recited like familiar prayers—we felt that our fathers had been perfect. Maggie and I are both hardcore "daddy's girls," our fathers pedestaled and protected in the sanctuaries of our hearts. Surely, however, both our fathers had faults? All humans do. But neither Maggie nor I had ever dared to consider this possibility until that day.

Reluctantly, we agreed to share a few things about our fathers that we believed were not perfect. Maggie went first, her words coming out in a pained whisper. Reluctantly, I followed suit, each admission feeling like a betrayal. Within a few minutes, we could not go on, but the truth had already been spoken. Now, we had to face it. The perfect fathers we had constructed existed only in our desperate need to believe in them.

Next came the most agonizing revelation of all. We realized we'd both been guilty of torturing our mothers in small and big ways. My heart constricted as memories flooded back, images I had conveniently buried. I knew my mother suffered from back pain all her life. I knew the reason was because she'd broken her tailbone giving birth to me. But I never gave her any consideration for that constant suffering. Perhaps I was too young to really understand, but deep down, I knew. I knew that if my brother and I roughhoused too long under her feet, especially on a hot summer day when her pain was at its worst, and especially after she'd issued several warnings to "take it outside," that the inevitable result would be that she would lose her temper. Nevertheless, in a misguided, desperate attempt to get her attention, I persisted. I pushed her to the edge, then acted shocked when she fell.

Maggie's eyes mirrored my own dawning understanding as she admitted similar truths. She knew that her father had not been the best husband, or even friend, to her mother. She knew that her mother had suffered for years trying to hold the family together, putting on a brave face while crumbling inside. And yet, Maggie had blamed her mother for the breakup with vicious teenage cruelty, while holding her father blameless. She had made her mother pay a thousand times for sins that weren't entirely hers.

But life, or fate, were not done with us that spring day. With hands that couldn't stop shaking, I showed Maggie the letter I'd written to my mother when I was in college—words of anger and blame that I could never take back, words that she carried to her grave. Maggie read it, handed it back, and stared at me, her face a mask of shock and recognition. And then she said, her voice barely audible, "Do you think it's possible our mothers were also victims, and that we contributed to their suffering?"

The answer was undeniable. Yes, we did. A long-held suppressed truth was revealed, and suddenly, we were both free. Standing there on that ordinary street corner on that extraordinary day, I whispered the words I wish I could have said to her face.

Forgive me, Mom.

CHAPTER 27

Angel Blessings

"Dogs are not our whole life, but they make our lives whole."
—Roger Caras

Maggie

It was just an ordinary day, until it wasn't. William had tossed and turned all night, his restless body somehow sensing what I couldn't yet see. William never slept well anyway, but this night felt different. It was heavier somehow, as if the air itself was dense with premonition. By morning, exhaustion had seeped into my bones, making my limbs feel like lead.

I awoke to Georgia's usual barking. A neighborhood cat had dared to slink across our sidewalk, and Georgia wouldn't stand for it. When I called to her, my voice still thick with sleep, she abandoned her post by the window and flew across the room. The mattress dipped as her warm little body nestled against mine. Her tail thumped against the sheets in a rhythm that had become the heartbeat of our home. I buried my fingers in her soft fur as she rolled over, exposing her belly for her morning ritual of rubs and kisses. Despite the rough night, in that moment, everything felt blissfully normal.

With Georgia's excited dance around my ankles, I dragged myself to the kitchen, the wooden floor cold beneath my bare feet. I prepared her breakfast, the clink of her food bowl against the tile floor sending her into a spinning frenzy of delight. Her nails clicked excitedly as she pranced around, waiting for that first delicious bite. After she devoured her meal, licking the bowl until it gleamed, I wrestled her into her jacket which was, as usual, a battle of wills that always ended with her dramatic sighs of resignation. She stood there, looking utterly betrayed, her tiny body rigid with indignation until I clipped on her leash. Then, as if a switch had flipped, she was once again my eager companion, tugging me toward the door, her body vibrating with anticipation.

Our morning walk followed the familiar path we'd traveled a thousand times before. Her ears perked up as we rounded the corner to what I'd nicknamed "Pomeranian Palace," the yard where four fluffy adversaries lived. Georgia's body tensed, her eyes narrowing with determination as she once again attempted to squeeze through the small gap in the fence. I could almost hear her thoughts: *The audacity of these creatures to exist in my neighborhood! Don't they know who I am?* I gently pulled her away, her reluctance evident in every backward glance she threw at the fence.

At the grocery store, Ally's face lit up when she saw us. "There's my favorite little lady!" she cooed, reaching beneath the counter for the special treats she kept just for Georgia. My little dog stood on her hind legs, front paws dancing in the air, eyes locked on Ally's hand with laser focus. The bond between them, this checkout girl and my tiny terror, never failed to make me smile. Georgia accepted her treat with the dignity of royalty receiving tribute, her tail wagging so hard her whole body shook.

Back at the apartment, Georgia charged up the stairs with boundless energy, her nails clicking against the stairs with the exact same rhythm they always did. She waited impatiently by our door, annoyed with me for taking too long. The moment I turned the key, she bolted inside, making a beeline for our bedroom where William lay. I heard her joyful leap onto the bed, followed by William's sleepy chuckle as she covered his face with tiny kisses.

The day moved forward like a familiar melody with each note exactly where it should be. But by afternoon, a discordant sound crept in, subtle at first but impossible to ignore. Outside, dogs barked their afternoon greetings, and the silence from within our apartment sent a chill through the air. Georgia, my little warrior, remained motionless on my pillow, her usual territorial barking conspicuously absent. When I sat down with a turkey sandwich, her favorite thing to beg for, she didn't even lift her head. Her eyes followed my movements, but her body remained still, as if held down by invisible weights.

I told myself she was just tired. I tried to push away the knot forming in my stomach. But as the hours crawled by and Georgia remained in her spot, that knot tightened, twisting my insides into painful shapes. Something was terribly wrong. I could feel it in the air, taste it in the back of my throat. It was a bitter foreboding that made my heart race.

For the rest of the afternoon, I watched her carefully, my eyes rarely leaving her small form. Every breath she took, every slight movement of her paws became a focus of my attention. I decided to feed her dinner early, hoping to prove my fears unfounded. The sound of her kibble hitting the metal bowl echoed through the apartment, a sound that had always sent her into a frenzy of excitement. My heart sunk when she merely lifted her head, her eyes meeting mine with a dullness that had never been there before, and then laid it back down without moving toward her food.

That's when I knew. The realization stole my breath. Georgia had been sick before, but it was rare, virtually unheard of for her to show no interest in food. She'd suffered from stomach issues and once battled a respiratory infection, but this was different. This was a dimming of her vibrant spirit.

I'd recently taken her to the vet for her regular checkup, so I knew she was up to date on vaccinations and treatments. When we'd rescued her during the dark days of the pandemic, she'd been a beacon of joy in our otherwise isolated world. The vet had estimated her age between five and seven years then, which would make her between nine and eleven now. She was no longer young, but not elderly either.

I researched her symptoms online, desperate for reassurance that this was something minor, something fixable. I clung to the memory of the last time I'd called the vet in panic, and how he'd gently reminded me, "Dogs get sick, too. Sometimes they have a bad day like we do." Maybe I was overreacting. Maybe tomorrow she'd be back to her bossy, energetic self. The thought provided a thin blanket of comfort.

I decided to take her for her evening walk, hoping the fresh air might revive her spirits. When I approached with her jacket, the one she usually fought against wearing, she sat perfectly still, allowing me to dress her without struggle. I immediately realized this was yet another sign that something was wrong. Outside, the cool night air seemed to offer her no comfort. She managed to squat and relieve herself, but then, in a move that sent ice through my veins, she simply sat down on the pavement, her eyes looking up at me with an expression that seemed to say, "I'm sorry, I just can't."

I scooped her up and carried her back upstairs. Her body felt different against my chest. She was heavier yet somehow diminished. With my heart pounding, I called the emergency vet's office.

The night assistant's voice was calm and professional as she suggested I monitor Georgia for an hour and see if I could get her to eat or drink. I brought out her favorite treats, the ones she would usually perform tricks for, and held my breath as she nibbled two without moving from her pillow. Then, miraculously, she barked at a passing dog. The sound, so normal and yet so precious in that moment, loosened the grip in my chest. Maybe she was just having an off day, after all.

Yet that nagging feeling, that terrible knowledge hovering at the edges of my consciousness, wouldn't release me. I sat beside her, my fingers gently stroking her fur, watching the rise and fall of her chest until her eyes closed and she drifted to sleep. Only then did I tear myself away to prepare William's dinner.

When I returned to the bedroom, Georgia's tiny chest was moving rapidly, too rapidly. Each breath seemed to require more effort than the last. Her heart was racing beneath my palm when I placed it gently on her side, though it seemed to calm slightly at my touch. I whispered soothing words, promises I wasn't sure I could keep, as I tried to convince myself that everything would be alright.

A noise from William's direction pulled my attention away, and my heart sank deeper as I realized he'd had an accident. The universe seemed determined to test my strength that night. With gentle hands and murmured reassurances, I helped him to the shower, the warm water washing away the physical evidence of his condition but doing nothing for the emotional toll it took on both of us. As I helped him into clean pajamas, his confused eyes kept darting to Georgia's small form on the bed. Even in his disoriented state, he sensed something was wrong.

Once William was settled back in bed, the lateness of the hour pressed down on me. I glanced at Georgia and saw her labored breathing had not improved. The rise and fall of her chest was erratic now, her body working too hard to perform this most basic function of life. I waited until William's breathing evened out in sleep before I called the emergency vet again. My voice broke as I described the deterioration in Georgia's condition.

The ride to the vet's office in the Uber was an eternity compressed into minutes. Georgia lay in my lap, her body so small against mine, her warmth seeping through my clothes and into my skin. I whispered a constant stream of love and reassurance into her ears, trying to keep the tremor from my voice. "You're going to be okay, Georgia. We're getting you help. You're the best dog in the whole world. You're my brave girl." Each word felt like a prayer, a desperate plea to whatever powers might be listening.

At 1:40 a.m., the sterile lights of the emergency vet's office made Georgia look even smaller, more vulnerable. The doctor took her from my arms with practiced gentleness, and I followed. I watched, vision blurring with unshed tears, as the doctor examined her. Georgia, my fierce, little warrior who normally had to be muzzled at the vet, didn't even raise her head in protest. That, more than anything, confirmed my worst fears.

After a flurry of injections and tests, the doctor placed her in an oxygen chamber. The glass between us might as well have been a chasm. Georgia looked so tiny, so fragile, curled up in the back of the chamber. When the vet approached me, his face wore the compassionate mask I'd seen before. I saw it when my father was dying and when William was diagnosed. It was the face of someone about to deliver news that would change everything.

Georgia's heart was failing. The words fell like stones, each one crushing something vital inside me. Chihuahuas typically have a temperature of one hundred degrees. Georgia's temperature was ninety-four because her heart could no longer regulate it. I looked at her. My companion, my friend, my comfort through so many dark days and I knew what I had to do. With a pain so deep it felt physical, I made the decision to say goodbye.

I carried her into a private room, her weight in my arms a precious burden I was not ready to relinquish. The vet provided a soft bed and, in a gesture that somehow broke my heart anew, a Hershey's kiss. He said that every dog deserves to taste chocolate once in its life. The sweet scent of the chocolate mingled with the antiseptic smell of the room as I cradled Georgia.

Words tumbled from my mouth then, a flood of gratitude and love. "Thank you for being the most wonderful dog in the world," I whispered, my voice thick with tears. "I love you so much, Georgia. I'm so grateful you came into my life when I needed you most." I told her how she had appeared at a time when my heart was desperate to care for something, to love something unconditionally. "You were everything I could have ever asked for. You more than I knew to ask for." I thanked her for being such a good seizure dog, for the countless times she had alerted me to William's condition, for the way she would lick his face after an episode to help bring him back. "I will miss you every day for the rest of my life," I promised, the words catching in my throat.

Then I just sat there with her in silence, trying to memorize everything about her—the pattern of her fur, the weight of her in my arms, the warmth of her body against mine. I wanted to freeze time, to stay in that moment forever rather than face what came next. But I couldn't. With trembling fingers, I reached for the little bell and rang it, the sound piercing the quiet room.

The vet returned, his movements gentle and practiced. Georgia didn't flinch when the needle went in. She died peacefully in my arms at 2:35 a.m., her last breath a soft sigh against my skin.

The world outside had transformed. As I left the vet alone, snow had begun to fall. They were delicate, silent flakes that seemed to absorb all sound. I stood there, face turned upward, letting the cold touch my skin, welcoming the numbness it brought. A car pulled up, and a woman burst out, clutching a dog to her chest as she rushed inside. My heart squeezed with empathy. I whispered a fervent prayer that her story would end differently than mine.

The Uber ride home was a blur of streetlights and tears. The driver, sensing my grief, shared that he had recently lost his own dog. We cried together, two strangers united by the profound love we had for our animals. How we love our pets with a purity and completeness that sometimes exceeds what we can offer each other.

As we neared home, dread consumed me. William. How could I tell William? Georgia had been his constant companion, his joy, his comfort through the fog of his condition. The thought of causing him this pain was almost unbearable. I prayed he would be asleep, giving me precious hours before I had to break his heart.

But William was awake when I returned, the building's live-in super, Buddy, sitting vigilantly by his side. He saw my empty arms and understood. His face crumpled, years seeming to add themselves to his features in seconds. That night, he succumbed to sleep through tears, his body trembling with each sob. In a small mercy, he had no seizures. I was grateful we would be spared another emergency room visit that night.

Morning brought fresh pain. William awoke calling for Georgia, his short-term memory erasing the heartbreak of the night before. I had to tell him again, watch him as he cried again. When he finally drifted back to sleep, I was grateful for the solitude, for the chance to grieve in my own head, with my own thoughts.

In the days that followed, the apartment was eerily quiet. The absence of Georgia's nails clicking on the floor, her barking at the window, her snoring beside me, created a silence that screamed. I didn't know how to navigate the world without her. Georgia had been my constant through some of the worst moments of my life. She was there when William received his diagnosis. She was there when my father took his last breath, her warm body pressed against my leg as I said goodbye. She was there on the day we buried him, her presence a balm to my raw grief.

For years, she was my best friend and the light of my life. That tiny terror, with her crossed eyes and bowed legs, had filled my heart in ways I never thought possible. And now she was gone, leaving behind a Georgia-shaped hole in our lives that nothing could ever fill.

CHAPTER 28

Welcome Home

*"And if, when it is all over, I'm asked what I did with my life,
I want to be able to say, I offered love."*
—Terri St. Cloud

Maggie

I knew I couldn't face the fluorescent lights and expectant faces of in-person classes that spring. I'd pinned my hopes on one Zoom class with Professor Saunders who was my rock, my academic lifeline, only to have him suddenly ripped away right after the semester started, his death yet another in my life. The class was cancelled. So close to graduation, 117 of the 120 credits dangling before me like a carrot just out of reach.

With no school that semester, I used my free time to visit my mother more often. As the ferry cut through the choppy waters from Manhattan to Staten Island, I pressed my forehead against the cold glass, my breath creating small clouds of fog that appeared and vanished with each exhale. The skyline receded behind me, and memories flooded in. The nights spent huddled in doorways, the gnawing emptiness of hunger that became a constant companion, the bone-deep cold that no amount of layers could keep at bay, the hands that hurt instead of helped. In those darkest moments, I never imagined I'd be here now, making weekly pilgrimages to see my mother, each visit a tentative stitch in our tattered relationship.

Despite the crushing loss of my father, Georgia and even my professor, William remained alive, a miracle I clung to. And somehow, against all odds, my mother and I were both healing, two wounded creatures finding their way back to each other.

The more time I spent with her, the more clarity emerged from the fog of our shared past. I'd always been searching, desperately hunting for maternal love in every relationship that came my way. The pattern was so clear now. There had been a constellation of women I'd latched onto, each one a potential substitute.

My aunt in New Orleans was the first star in this constellation, shining brightest in my childhood memories. I worshipped her. Her home in New Orleans became my sanctuary, a place where childhood summers unfolded with a magic entirely absent from my daily life. The moment I was old enough to fly alone, I spent the summers with her and my cousins.

New Orleans wrapped around me like a warm embrace. Our relationship blossomed into everything I yearned for but couldn't find with my own mother. In her sunlit kitchen, she taught me how to cook and bake. We made rainbow cookies that painted our fingers with food coloring, and chocolate soufflés. We gathered around her table every evening, savoring not just the food but genuine conversation. No screaming pierced those walls. No bitter critiques of my shortcomings poisoned the air. We attended temple each weekend, and for the first time, I felt the spiritual connection of my faith and a sense of belonging.

After a few golden summers, my aunt extended an invitation to me to enroll in the prestigious private school my cousins attended. The possibility dazzled and terrified me in equal measure. To live that charmed existence every single day? To wake up in their stunning home, surrounded by wealth and comfort and, most precious of all, unconditional acceptance?

But the thought of leaving my father carved a hollow space in my chest I couldn't ignore. Despite everything, I missed my mother and sister, too, when I was away. The familiar dysfunction was still home.

My parents, especially my mother, were not thrilled with the idea. Once they vetoed the idea, my New Orleans summers evaporated like the morning mist. Our connection faded to occasional phone calls and stilted exchanges at family gatherings, each one a reminder of what might have been.

The void remained until Cindy appeared. The jewelry-making, weed-selling, embodiment of everything cool and rebellious. Her hippie spirit seemed ageless, a portal to a freedom I desperately craved.

When she banished me for stealing her weed, the hunger returned. I then found two mothers named Cathy. I'm not sure if it was cosmic coincidence or desperate pattern-seeking. Toni's mother welcomed me with open arms, her only-child household brightened by my presence. She granted us liberties I'd never known, a taste of the autonomy I craved.

Rachel's mother, the real estate agent who helped my sister and me find our first apartment, arrived next. She dazzled me with her competence and class, a blueprint for the woman I might become if given half a chance.

Then came Kerri, just down the street, her proximity and permission bundled into one convenient package. She let me smoke cigarettes under her roof and trusted me with her children, offering payment that felt like validation.

The list went on and on. Audrey, Charlie's mother; Melody, her daughter-in-law; scattered others whose kindness I clung to like a lifeline. The pattern repeated with painful predictability, each relationship a temporary balm on a wound that would not heal.

The supreme irony came when I finally acquired a "real" second mother through marriage—my mother-in-law, with whom I shared very little. After a lifetime of collecting maternal figures, the one legitimately bestowed upon me through family bonds remained a stranger, our relationship a minefield neither of us cared to navigate.

And then…Traci. Meeting her that day on the sidewalk, I couldn't have known she would become my compass, the one that would guide me home. Her wisdom, humor, and radical acceptance transformed me in ways I'm still discovering. Her compassion planted the seed that grew into my determination to heal my relationship with my own mother. The village that raised me was imperfect, but without it, I might never have found my way back to where I am now. I hope someday to be for someone else what these women were for me; a lighthouse in the storm.

All these relationships except the one with Traci had faded long ago, but I had my mother again. Our weekly conversations gradually deepened, revealing layers of understanding I'd never thought possible between us.

Curiosity about her perspective on my homelessness gnawed at me. Fear of disrupting our fragile peace made me hesitate, but the questions burned inside me, demanding answers.

The opening came unexpectedly. We sat at her kitchen table, the newspaper spread between us like neutral territory, when an article about New York City's migrant crisis caught my eye. The image of families huddled on sidewalks outside overcrowded shelters made my throat tighten.

"Those poor children," I murmured, the memory of bone-chilling nights rising, unbidden. "I can't imagine them shivering out there."

My mother's response stunned me. "I can't imagine anyone having to sleep on the street," she said softly, her eyes not meeting mine. "I don't know how you ever survived it."

The mention of my homelessness, a subject we had danced around for years, sent a jolt through me. I seized the moment. "How did you feel when you found out I was living on the streets?"

Her hands shook slightly as she folded the newspaper. When she spoke, raw honesty filled the space between us.

"I was so furious I couldn't see straight when we first found out you'd been evicted from the apartment we rented for you." Pain etched lines around her mouth. "We knew you were struggling, but your father and I had no idea you desperately needed help. We thought you'd gone crazy, abandoned your family to party with your cousin."

She took a deep breath. "When your father and I heard about the damage Rick had done to the apartment, and the cost to repair it, I was done with you. I demanded your father cut off all contact." Her voice cracked. "My anger blinded me. Then you disappeared. That was the first time I became afraid."

Her candor pierced me. My mother's default had always been anger, yet hearing she'd been angry enough to erase me from her life felt like a physical blow. As a mother myself, I couldn't fathom my children doing anything so terrible I'd never want to see them again.

Yet, I had done exactly that to my mother. The realization crashed over me like an icy wave. My actions hadn't just shattered my life; they'd ripped through hers as well. In my desperation and anger at being abandoned, I'd never considered how my disappearance had wounded others.

"I'm so sorry, Mom," I whispered, tears burning behind my eyes. "I never really thought about how my being on the streets affected you."

Gratitude softened her features. "Thank you. I understand how your daily struggle to survive clouded out other concerns." She twisted her wedding ring, a nervous habit I'd forgotten. "I wanted to find you but had no idea how. You had no phone, didn't answer emails. No one knew where you were." Her voice dropped to a whisper. "All I could hope was that you'd eventually call for help, which is how I finally found out where you were."

"When was that?"

A sad smile touched her lips. "It's actually a funny story. I went to Publix for groceries and saw your father standing at the Western Union line. I knew immediately he was sending you money." Her eyes grew distant. "He looked so defeated when he told me you were living on the streets."

She shook her head. "I was so shocked I just walked away to do my shopping. I'd always known you might be homeless, but I hadn't allowed myself to imagine what that really meant." Her voice dropped. "I survived by not thinking about it. Even when your children visited us in Florida, we never spoke your name. You were the elephant in the room. I even took down your pictures to avoid stirring painful memories."

Her words sliced through me. I'd known my children visited my parents, and I'd been grateful they maintained that connection when I couldn't. But I'd never considered the emotional gymnastics required to host my children while erasing all traces of me. Had they asked questions? The thought of their confusion and hurt made me ache, but I couldn't bring myself to ask.

"The years you spent on the street weren't sad ones for us, but they certainly weren't happy either," she continued. "We went about our lives, but you were never far from my thoughts, whether I wanted you there or not." She wiped her eyes. "Your father had a much harder time than I did because my anger protected me from feeling the full weight of your absence. He didn't have that luxury."

Her face softened. "I knew he was helping you, even when he wouldn't admit it. Part of me was furious with him for making things easier for you." She paused, vulnerability shining in her eyes. "But another part found comfort knowing there were nights you were warm and safe."

Her confession haunted me for days afterward. Gratitude for her honesty mingled with a flash of anger I had no right to feel. The following week, I gathered my courage and decided to reciprocate her honesty, to share the truth she still didn't know. I didn't want to bring up bad memories, but there was one thing I was adamant about. She needed to know that I had not just abandoned my children.

"Mom, there's something you need to know."

She waited, tension filling the space between us.

"When I first left the house, I asked my husband to come with me, but he declined."

Confusion crossed her face. "Why would he do that?"

"I was in bad shape, and we both thought it would be better if I got sober and then came back." My voice wavered. "But that never happened because Rick showed up, and even though I'd stopped drinking, I was now smoking weed daily."

"But many people smoke weed, right?" she offered, surprising me with her attempt at understanding.

"Yes, that's true," I admitted. "And I did ask to go back a few times, but I was not given another chance."

My confession changed nothing tangible, yet unburdening myself felt like setting down a weight I'd carried for years. Silence stretched between us, my mother's gaze fixed on some distant point.

When she finally spoke, her words nearly stopped my heart.

"What happened to you with the children wasn't right."

Blood rushed in my ears. "What did you say, Mom?"

She turned to me, her eyes glistening. "You had a lot of issues, and you were horrible that last time you visited us in Florida. You drank every drop of liquor in your father's cabinet and barely paid attention to us." She reached across the table, her fingers briefly brushing mine. "But you were always a good mother and adored your children."

Emotion surged through me, threatening to overflow. For the first time, my mother had acknowledged that perhaps everything wasn't entirely my fault. That I too had been a victim in some way. Her recognition that I hadn't failed as a mother healed something I'd thought permanently broken. Fighting back tears, I thanked her quietly for listening to my side of the story.

"I know this has been an absolutely horrible situation for you," I said, my voice thick with emotion. "You lost precious time with your grandchildren because of my actions, and I am so deeply sorry." My throat tightened as I continued. "When I think about the time Daddy could have spent with the kids, it makes me physically ill. I made so many mistakes, and I'm sorry you had to suffer for them." Tears finally spilled over. "I just want you to know that I've suffered for it every single day. I know you haven't forgiven me and I haven't forgiven myself, either."

She squeezed my hand, her touch a balm I'd craved for decades. "I understand, Maggie. Don't worry. Everything will work out in the end."

For the first time in years, I believed her.

I could see her discomfort with the emotional intensity, so I stood and wrapped my arms around her thin shoulders. She hugged me back, her embrace tentative at first, then tightening as if afraid I might slip away again. Against my ear, she whispered the words I'd been waiting a lifetime to hear.

"I'm glad you're back, Maggie. Welcome home."

Maggie in Brooklyn

Epilogue

*"To be what we are, and to become what we are capable
of becoming, is the only end of life."*
—Robert Louis Stevenson

March 22, 2025, Traci

This story ended exactly five years after it began. It was my grandmother's birthday again. As I stared at her picture, lost in thought, something unexpected caught my eye. My granddaughter's eyes are the same as hers. The same delicate, slightly oblong, shape. The same quiet intensity, reminding me of the long-term tenacity of DNA. Hope is the same. It waits; it endures.

For weeks I'd tried to write this epilogue, the words refusing to come. Maggie had come so far, but her struggle continued. William wasn't just unwell. He was dying and could not be left alone, even for a few minutes. I watched helplessly as Maggie's life slowly devolved into the all-consuming role of caregiver, her own dreams fading into the background, her only respite those brief, stolen visits to her mother that left her both nourished and drained. Even reading through the final draft of this book had been a juggling act, squeezed into those rare moments when William slept.

A difficult choice loomed ahead—placing William in assisted living. The decision would not be easy. Maggie still saw the man who had pulled her out of the shadows and back into light when no one else would. How do you repay such a debt?

Adding to her challenges, despite having 117 credits, Maggie still needed three specific classes to graduate—three more mountains to climb—due to the specific requirements of the English major. However, very few online courses were available and making it to campus was impossible.

Discouraged for Maggie—and to be honest, for myself—I picked up a copy of *Unsheltered Love* and flipped to the quote on the last page from the film *The Innocents*: *Faith is twenty-four hours of doubt and one minute of hope*. We needed that one minute.

I reminded myself where Maggie was at the end of 2021, before she went back to Brooklyn College, before *Unsheltered Love* defied all odds to become a *Wall Street Journal* and *USA Today* bestseller, before we won the Eric Hoffer grand prize, and before we completed this book.

Still, the question of how, or even if, Maggie could finish her degree continued to nag me. And then a small opening. Could Maggie change her major from English to General Studies? If it wasn't too late, then she would only need one more class to graduate. One more class instead of three. That felt possible.

Hope rushed in. Maggie, her eyes suddenly alight with possibility, immediately registered for an online class for the first summer session. Monday morning, we met with her advisor on a Zoom call and learned the news we feared—Brooklyn College did not offer a general studies major. Hope evaporated as quickly as it appeared, leaving behind the all-too-familiar taste of disappointment

I told her not to worry—that even if she never graduated—she'd already climbed mountains. Maggie nodded with a brave smile that didn't quite reach her eyes, but then reminded me that she had to do this for the one person who'd always been her lighthouse in the storm.

Her father.

The next day, Maggie spoke to the head of the English department. And then, one last miracle. There was another online class offered the second summer session and one more in the fall, both of which would fulfill her two remaining requirements.

Sometimes, when the odds against us tower like insurmountable walls, and the world seems determined to break you, the heart is left with just one choice. It has to be stronger. It must beat louder. It needs to love harder. Because sometimes, that's all we have.

Maggie trying on her cap and gown

◆ ◆ ◆

*It's not the critic who counts, not the man who points out how
the strong man stumbles. The credit belongs to the man who is
actually in the arena…who strives valiantly, who errs…because
there is no effort without error and shortcoming…who at the best
in the end knows the triumph of high achievement, and who at
the worst, if he fails, at least fails while daring greatly, so that his
place shall never be with those cold and timid souls who neither
know victory nor defeat.*
—Theodore Roosevelt

Traci Medford-Rosow is a *Wall Street Journal* and *USA Today* bestselling author of three published books. The first, *Inflection Point: War and Sacrifice in Corporate America*, was published by Pegasus Books in 2015. The second, *Unblinded: One Man's Courageous Journey through Darkness to Sight*, was published by Morgan James in 2018. The third, *Unsheltered Love: Homelessness, Hunger, and Hope in a City Under Siege*, was published by Morgan James in 2022. *Chasing Light: Two Women, Their Mothers, and a Secret That Changed Their Lives* is her fourth nonfiction title.

In addition to being named to *USA Today*, *Unblinded* is also a *Publishers Weekly*, *Indie Bound*, Amazon and Barnes and Noble bestseller. *Unblinded* was also named to Kirkus Reviews' Best Books of 2020. *Unsheltered Love* is a *Wall Street Journal*, *USA Today*, Amazon Charts, and Barnes & Nobel #1 bestseller. It is also the winner of the 2023 Eric Hoffer Grand Prize.

Traci lives in New York City with her husband. They have two adult children.

Contact Traci at www.tracimedfordrosow.com.

Maggie Wright is the co-author of the bestseller, *Unsheltered Love: Homelessness, Hunger, and Hope in a City Under Siege*. *Chasing Light: Two Women, Their Mothers, and a Secret That Changed Their Lives* is her second nonfiction title.

Maggie lives in Brooklyn with her partner and two beloved cats. Contact Maggie at MaggieWrightAuthor@gmail.com

Appendix A

Excerpt from *Unsheltered Love, Homelessness,
Hunger and Hope in a City under Siege.*

Selected Praise for *Unsheltered Love*
"When COVID-19 struck, we were told to shelter in place for a
"couple of weeks" until the surge passed. Regardless of that mis-
calculation and government overreach, what if one didn't have a
home to take cover from the virus? The oft out of sight became
invisible, more isolated and vulnerable than ever before, but the
plight of humanity did not disappear because we suddenly couldn't
see it. Challenging and inspiring, this is the story of one couple
that made a difference in the lives of the homeless in New York
City during the darkest days of the pandemic. Medford-Rosow
poignantly shares the daily struggle of those on the street and how
their heartbreak and misery touched her heart in incredible ways.
Choosing to make a difference in an impactful way, the author
and her husband invested time, energy, finances, and love into
the lives of the less fortunate and helped to lift several above their
dire realities. Interspersed narratives from the homeless shape the
humanity of those we often pass on the street without a glance,
but it is hope and love that are the essence of this story, powering
it through not the worst but the best humanity has to offer."
—*The Eric Hoffer Award*

"With a pandemic raging, our nation's cities under siege and residents sheltered in place, Traci Medford-Rosow and her husband, Joel, see what no one else was looking for—homeless men and women--and take a leap of faith to show the unsheltered love. Daily walks in their neighborhood led them to become involved with new friends that most in their city shunned and even feared. Traci became especially close to a battered and abused homeless woman named Maggie while Joel dreamed of a city where no one goes hungry or sleeps on the streets. Handing out homemade sandwiches to strangers, they did not look away from distress. While nobody can help everybody, they proved that everybody can help somebody. As you turn the pages of this well-written and hopeful story, keep an open mind and eyes for ways to make a difference. Unsheltered Love is worthy of your time."

–Ron Hall, #1 *New York Times* bestselling
author of *Same Kind of Different as Me*, *Workin'
Our Way Home* and *What Difference do it Make?*

"Medford-Rosow relates the stories of several people in New York City who were homeless at the start of the COVID pandemic. In March 2020, the author and her husband noticed the increased number of unhoused people living on the streets of their New York City neighborhood. Concerned about their survival, Medford-Rosow brought them sandwiches regularly and gradually befriended several. She tells each person's story, focusing on how they came to be homeless and the efforts to find them social services and a room. The stories of the unhoused people are contrasted with events from the author's own life, demonstrating that the circumstances that cause people to lose their homes are not uncommon. At the end of each chapter, Maggie Wright, one of Medford-Rosow's unhoused friends, gives her perspective on the chapter's events, providing additional insight. The author ponders the impact that the first year of the pandemic and New York City's COVID policies had on the unhoused population. VERDICT: A moving account of the experience of unhoused people in a major American city."

–Library Journal

"Revealing the power of being present and listening to others, Traci Medford-Rosow's memoir Unsheltered Love covers her encounters with people facing homelessness during COVID-19. In the early days of the pandemic, Medford-Rosow and her husband Joel began taking walks to give food and supplies to homeless people near their home in New York City. Along the way, they listened to people's stories and grappled with their own privilege and desire to create lasting change. Across a year and half span, Medford-Rosow shares the stories of those she interacted with, including Maggie Wright, whose clear, honest voice and willingness to share her story is a gift. Her journal entries reveal her pain, hope, how she learned to trust again, and how she began rebuilding all she'd lost. Moved along by engaging conversations that reveal both Medford-Rosow's perspective and the perspectives of Maggie and other homeless people, the book includes insights about life on the streets, where money helps to buy food, but also when it comes to buying a cup of coffee in order to use the bathroom at McDonald's. So, too, are there grueling truths about what it means to try to help, and about how investments of time and money often yield few results. Still, the book is generous with hope—both from Medford-Rosow and from the people she's met. Medford-Rosow is humble in revealing what she had to learn the hard way: the book's late updates on the people covered herein include both positive developments and evidence that not everyone makes it through. Unsheltered Love is a moving memoir about pandemic connections formed with people facing homelessness."

–Foreword Reviews "

A New Yorker connects with her unhoused neighbors in this memoir. Medford-Rosow's story of developing meaningful personal relationships with houseless people who spent their days near her Manhattan home is effectively a 2020 time capsule. It recounts the changes that Covid-19 brought to New York City and offers a humane account of the realities that people without housing face. The sudden shutdown of many local businesses in March 2020 meant that local panhandlers had few donors, so Medford-Rosow and her husband, Joel, began taking daily walks through their neighborhood, first offering people dollar bills and then homemade sandwiches. Over time, they developed close relationships with several people, got to know their stories, and supported them as they tried to move into sheltered housing. Medford-Rosow connected most deeply with a woman who served as this book's developmental editor and contributed short essays to the text under the pseudonym Maggie Wright; in them, she writes about the same events as the author but from her own perspective. In these pages, Medford-Rosow writes about emotional moments with an admirable lack of sentimentality. Throughout, she takes pains not to portray herself and Joel as heroic—for instance, she still worries that the city's plan to use nearby hotels as shelters will hurt local property values—and she offers no broad policy recommendations. Instead, Maggie's personal journey, with its many setbacks and successes, serves as the book's core, and it's an effective one; her middle-class background and struggles with addiction are likely to resonate with many readers. The book also does an effective job of evoking the uncertainty of the early days of the Covid-19 pandemic, from the initial assumptions that offices would only be closed briefly to phases of reopening to premature claims of victory as the first wave receded. A focused and engaging remembrance of a specific community changed by the Covid-19 pandemic."

—Kirkus Reviews

PROLOGUE

The first time I saw Maggie she was busy sweeping the most unlikely place—the sidewalk on the corner of Park Avenue and 30th Street. New York City's natural hum seemed to go silent as I paused to take in her appearance: tattered clothes, dirty stocking cap, shifting gaze. But it was her hands that held my attention. Covered in grime, tightly gripping the handle of a broken broom, she was intent on sweeping the area around her makeshift home, as if this one vestige of domesticity might keep her from falling into the abyss that had become her reality.

I reached into the back pocket of my jeans for a few dollars. As she accepted the offering from my outstretched hand, our eyes met. I could see her inner light flickering for an instant, defying her broken appearance before she turned and walked away.

What was it that made me stop and look at her, this one particular woman on this one particular day? I'd seen so many homeless people in the city that spring. I told myself there was not much I could do to help. Especially now. Especially in the middle of a raging pandemic. I assuaged my guilt by giving a few dollars to some of the men and women I passed by.

As one day melded into the next, I began having difficulty sleeping. Tossing all night in my comfortable bed, I knew I should share the truth about the plight of the homeless men and women who had no beds that spring—the relentless winter cold, their hunger, the ambulance sirens that disturbed their fragile sleep, and their fear, which was as contagious as the virus itself.

The divisive nature of the pandemic was evident from the beginning. Once fellow comrades in battle, as the weeks and months passed, friends, and even family members, became potential sources of the virus. The homeless, due to their living conditions, were especially feared.

Still, somehow, in the midst of the suffering, the starvation and deaths we would witness, the personal tragedies we would face, there endured a fragile and elusive, yet omnipresent, hope.

And in the center of that hope, there was love.

CHAPTER 1

The Gathering Storm

On March 18, 2020, we entered the nearly-deserted airport lobby. No one was even waiting in the security line. But the airport employees were there behind the check-in counters. They did not have a choice. No work meant no paycheck, which, for many locals, meant no food.

My husband, Joel, and I had been on vacation in Turks & Caicos. Just a few days earlier, the only concern I'd had was putting on enough sunscreen to ensure that my sun-damaged, freckled skin would not burn. Before the day was over, however, that reality had disappeared when rumors of an allegedly deadly virus, food shortages, and imminent border closings started circulating up and down the expansive Grace Bay beach.

We'd discussed the pros and cons of staying on the island versus returning home. Home was New York City—the nation's first epicenter of COVID-19. The island's borders were still open, but we saw the first signs of panic buying. Turks was dependent on supplies arriving by plane or ship, and both forms of travel were being cancelled on a daily basis.

Our daughter, Kyra, suggested we should consider coming home before the borders closed. Our son, Chad, was worried that if we did return, one or both of us would get COVID. We weighed the odds of getting stuck in a place with insecure food supplies versus catching the virus in New York.

The decision was binary—stay or leave.

We decided to take our chances in New York City and waited patiently to board one of the last aircrafts that was allowed on the small island before its borders closed. The boarding process lasted only a few minutes.

Even though "social distancing" had not yet become a household term, it was a reality as we flew home in silence. Despite the quiet, there was a discernible negative energy on the plane—a mixture of fear, panic and irritation.

Three hours later, we landed at John F. Kennedy International Airport. By the time we disembarked, there were almost 3,000 cases of coronavirus in the city, 463 people had been hospitalized and twenty had died. Getting through Customs and Immigration took less than a minute. That airport was deserted too.

"Welcome home," the immigration inspector said, greeting us with a somber smile. "You made it."

"Is it as bad as people are saying?" I asked, afraid of his answer.

"Even worse," he replied.

We headed toward the empty taxicab line and jumped into the first one we saw. Our driver appeared confused and disheveled. Oh boy, I thought as we made our way home through the deserted highways and streets. A journey that often took over an hour was less than twenty minutes. *Here we go. It's going to be a bumpy ride.*

When we pulled up in front of our apartment on 38th Street, the building was dark and lifeless. All but two of our co-op's nine residents had left the city for surrounding areas that were perceived to be safer. I tossed my suitcase on the bed, changed into my pajamas and headed toward the living room at the front of our apartment. I looked out the window at the once thriving, now deserted Park Avenue. The city had a gray, ghost-like appearance and feel, almost as if it were the aftermath of a war. Still. Lifeless.

An eerie silence blanketed the streets and sidewalks. A lone pigeon landed on my windowsill and stared at me. The bird's eyes held an expression I did not recognize at the time, but would come to know from the squirrels' faces I would see in the deserted parks in the coming weeks and months.

Hunger. The animals in New York City are dependent on people eating—and dropping—food in the parks, on the sidewalks, in the streets. They are not domesticated animals, yet they are not quite wild, either.

As I fell asleep that night, I was afraid of the dark for the first time since I was a young girl. Despite my fear, however, I was aware that I was lucky. I was warm and safe, unlike the group of homeless people I'd seen bedding down for the night by the church on our street corner.

The next morning, even before I'd finished unpacking, I went out to buy some eggs and milk. Walking through the streets, I saw few cars and even fewer pedestrians. Most stores, other than the groceries and pharmacies, were closed, many were boarded up. It wasn't necessary to stop for traffic at a street corner; I could cross in any direction—even diagonally—without waiting for the *Walk* sign to appear.

What I did see, however, were homeless men and women. *Were there actually more than usual or was I just noticing them because there were so few other people?* As I passed by, I paused to look at their faces. Crooked grimaces revealed their truths—hunger, confusion, fear. By the time I returned home I felt unsettled, although I was unsure why.

I tried to focus on small tasks that afternoon, but the images of the homeless men and women distracted me—their dirty faces, empty panhandling cups, tattered clothes. With so little foot traffic in the city, their ability to beg for money was virtually eliminated. It occurred to me that while I and most of my colleagues were able to continue working remotely, so many vulnerable citizens were cut off from any possibility of making a living—restaurant workers, hair stylists, manicurists, gig workers, and also panhandlers—people who did not earn a salary, rather were paid by the job, the hour, the tip, the handout.

Even before the pandemic, before the protests, before George Floyd's graphic death, the inequality between the haves and have-nots had become a weekly topic of conversation in our house. Joel and I had numerous discussions about the country becoming a two-tier society in which the rich were getting richer and the poor even poorer. Nevertheless, I didn't know what I was going to do about any of it that afternoon.

But what I did know—what we all knew—was that the virus was real and it was in the center of our world. New York alone had more cases, more hospitalizations and more deaths than any other place on the planet. And half of the state's cases were clustered in the city—on our streets, in our buildings, in our homes.

What I also knew was that while being homeless in New York City was never an easy life, during the pandemic it had become a challenge to even eat, much less survive.

I awoke the next morning to another brutally cold day. Despite being the first day of spring, New York City was still in the grip of winter. In fairness, the city is not known for the beauty of its springs. Many years the winter turns to summer in a week's time. Nevertheless, despite having lived there for over forty years, I was not used to it, having grown up in Virginia where spring arrives by early March.

Joel and I had met the summer before I started law school in his office—in his actual office—in Washington, D.C. He was a federal mediator working at the Federal Mediation and Conciliation Service. I was a first-year law student. I'd landed a summer job tabulating labor statistics, and Joel's office had an extra desk in it. Before the summer was over, we'd become a couple. When Joel was reassigned to the New York City office, I transferred schools, and we packed up our few possessions and headed north.

Now, after forty-three years in the city, we were New Yorkers. We set out from our apartment that early spring morning with no destination or specific purpose in mind. As had become our custom when taking walks, we took a few dollars from the jar on our kitchen counter where we kept single bills for tips.

Even before the pandemic, there was an on-going debate about giving money to the homeless. Some New Yorkers were against it, believing the money was used to buy drugs and booze. The other contingent believed that a few dollars here and there was a good compromise between supporting possible bad habits and just walking by the most vulnerable city residents without an acknowledgement of their suffering.

After only three blocks, our pockets were empty. Again, I wondered whether there were actually more homeless people in our neighborhood, or if the near total desertion of the city streets made their presence more obvious. Regardless, we needed more dollars, but not a single bank was opened.

The outside ATMs were available, but the smallest bill distributed was a five. I didn't think Joel would support this expenditure, and to be honest, I was not comfortable with that amount, either. I proposed a compromise.

"Let's get twenty five-dollar bills. When they're gone, we'll call it a day."

"That's a good plan," Joel agreed.

An hour later, our pockets empty, we headed home. Joel voiced what I was thinking.

"I've never seen so many homeless people."

"I know. I noticed them yesterday when I went to the grocery store."

The next day we debated going out again. Joel was not as eager as I was. "We're supposed to be sheltering-in-place."

"I know, except Governor Cuomo specifically said we were allowed to go out for exercise. We're walking. We're exercising."

"I don't think we should be out on the streets so much. What if one of us catches the virus?"

"The chances of us catching the virus on the deserted streets is not very high. Besides, you've seen the homeless people. They're hungry. What are our options? I mean, really, what choice do we have?"

"Yeah, I agree. But every time we go out on the streets we're taking a risk."

"I know. But every time we don't go out on the streets, some of them will not eat that day. I have to live with myself when this is over. If we weren't here in the middle of it all, it might be different. We wouldn't see it. But we are here, and we do see it. I can't just watch them starve from the safety of our windows and do nothing."

Joel sighed. A deep, prolonged, mournful sigh. "How long do you propose keeping this routine up?"

"Until the streets are not so deserted and the homeless can panhandle again."

"Okay, so just to be clear, this is not our permanent new mission, right?"

"No, I don't think my feet or my wallet could survive that," I said in an effort to lighten the mood. In my heart, however, I knew we were in it for the long haul. I never felt it was our sole responsibility to take care of the homeless population during the pandemic, but I also knew they needed the support of every person who was willing to help.

Joel and I were just two ordinary people. And we were scared.

But the circumstances were extraordinary.

We continued to roam the city every morning handing out a few dollars to each homeless man or woman we passed. Most days we'd walk five to eight miles depending on the route we took and how sore our legs and feet were. In the afternoons, I'd do my legal work and Joel, a licensed mental health counselor, held video sessions with his clients.

On Friday, March 27 at 7:00 p.m., we had just settled down in our living room to watch *Jeopardy* when we heard a roar outside our windows. I jumped off the sofa and stuck my head out the window. Above the deserted street, person after person leaned out their windows, clapping and screaming *Thank you!* to New York City's health care workers. I was surprised at the number of people I saw. Up until that moment, I'd thought the city was virtually deserted.

As the nightly tributes continued, the noise increased. People banged on pots and pans, shouted through megaphones and blew through toy horns. Those two minutes of tribute became the highlight of our day, reminding us that thousands of essential workers were risking their lives to protect ours. The scene was nothing short of bone-chilling. I grabbed my phone and captured it on video to remind myself of the sacrifices being made by so many.

The following morning, we set out in a westward direction and then uptown toward Times Square, which was eerily quiet and empty. Other than the homeless, we did not see another New Yorker.

An hour later, we passed by the closed New York City Public Library on Fifth Avenue at 42nd Street. The library is an imposing white structure, reminiscent of a temple in ancient Rome, replete with enormous columns and two statues of lions seemingly guarding each side of the entrance. I wondered how many other times since it was established in 1895 it had been shut down. Even though closed, it wasn't deserted—there were numerous homeless people sitting on its steps and at little tables surrounding the exterior, most with dazed looks on their hungry faces.

We were trying to socially distance as we walked the streets, so rather than go into the enclosed area I leaned over the concrete balustrade surrounding the library and offered a few dollars to the homeless man sitting at a nearby table. He accepted the money with a confused yet grateful smile. He immediately stood up. I watched him walk across the street to a bodega, one of the few that were open that March.

As we made our way toward our apartment, we saw a homeless man urinating into an abandoned phone booth, and another, pants halfway down with his back propped up against a building wall for support, defecating. I'd seen my fair share of men urinating on the city sidewalks, but I'd never seen anything like this. I wondered if the men were freely relieving themselves because the streets were deserted or because everything was closed and there were no available public bathrooms.

"Oh boy," I said as we skittered by. "This situation is getting worse by the day." Joel, uncharacteristically silent, only nodded.

After walking two blocks farther east, we were back on Park Avenue. I spotted another man bent over inside an old phone booth. *Oh my. Not another one.* As we approached him, however, it became clear that he was not urinating. Sensing our presence, he turned around, and needle still in his left arm, collapsed to the sidewalk. As his eyes rolled back in his head, he started foaming from the mouth.

Joel ran down the street looking for a policeman. I called 911. My call was answered immediately. As I hung up, I spotted Joel running back up Park Avenue, panting and out of breath.

"I couldn't find a policeman," he shouted.

"That's okay. I got right through to 911. An ambulance is on its way."

At the time, empty ambulances were stationed every few blocks to answer emergency calls from virus victims. Two minutes later one pulled up to where we were standing. We knew the paramedics would not want or need our further help. We pointed to the man on the ground and left. As I crossed the street, I looked back over my shoulder and saw one paramedic on his knees administering mouth-to-mouth to the victim while his partner appeared to be checking the man's vital signs.

"God help us all," I said over and over as I stumbled home. It would become my mantra for the next one hundred days.

Thankfully, I had no way of knowing that what we witnessed that morning would become our new normal or that our finely-constructed reality would soon shatter.

Maybe it was a curse. Maybe it was a blessing. It would be a long time before I had an answer. And when it came, unbidden but welcome, it would cause me to question every truth I'd held self-evident.

◆ ◆ ◆

I was so cold.

So hungry. There was no food. No money. How were we going to survive this? If we didn't die from the virus, we'd certainly starve to death.

Maggie Wright, March 2020

CHAPTER 2

March Madness

By the end of March, we both knew that we needed to concentrate our efforts to aid the homeless on a smaller area of the city. "We're spreading ourselves too thin by walking helter-skelter and not really making a difference to anyone," I said.

Joel agreed. "So, where do you want to go?"

"I've seen a lot of homeless people on Park Avenue between our apartment and 30th Street."

"Really? What do they look like?"

"Well, there's that young, red-headed man in his late twenties or early thirties who panhandles on 37th Street—the tall guy with the sign that reads *homeless and hungry*."

"Oh, I know who you mean, but it looks like something isn't quite right with him."

"I'm guessing that most people don't end up homeless if everything is okay in their lives."

"That's true." Joel agreed. "Who else?"

"There's that couple who have created a makeshift home on the corner of Park and 30th."

"Which couple?"

"They're white. She's very short. He's about average height. Look to be in their thirties or forties. And their friend who often hangs out with them—the nice-looking Black man who is always smiling."

"Oh, right, I know who you mean."

"And just one block south in those abandoned phone booths is an older Black man sitting with a blanket on his lap, and a young Black woman is often next to him."

"Right, I know the man you are referring to. He's the one who says 'much appreciated' when you put a dollar in his cup." Joel said. "Do you think they actually live in those telephone booths?"

"I think so. It seems like all their stuff is in bags beside them. The other day I noticed the woman pulling a folding chair down from the top of the telephone booth. I guess that is where she stores it when she leaves."

"And sometimes there is that middle-aged, very thin, Hispanic man who walks by and talks to them for a few minutes."

"The guy who is always moving around so fast with his arms flapping?" Joel asked.

"Yes, he's the one. So why don't we concentrate our efforts on those ten blocks of Park Avenue?

"Okay, that sounds like a good plan," Joel agreed.

Park Avenue is one of the nicest streets in Manhattan and one of the few with traffic running in both directions. A combination of residential buildings and retail spaces border the wide, tree-lined boulevard, which stretches down to Union Square Market on 14th Street, twenty-four blocks south of where we live. During the first month of the pandemic, the market became a resting spot and a respite for us during our long walks. There were merchants selling farm-grown, spring vegetables, honey, cheese, apples, and farm-raised meat and fish.

There were also other New Yorkers strolling around the market, and for the most part, they did not appear to be afraid of an outdoor venue. Dr. Fauci had advised the general public *not* to wear masks claiming, "There is no reason to be walking around with a mask," and the Surgeon General, Jerome Adams, agreed, declaring, "Stop buying masks! They are not effective in preventing the general public from catching #Coronavirus." In light of this advice, we could see people's faces, and we smiled at one another as we passed by, resolute and determined, despite the obvious concern we all shared.

On Monday morning, March 30th, we headed downtown where we heard a distant roar from the New York City Harbor. The promised Navy hospital ship, the *USNS Comfort*, arrived to great fanfare and, unfortunately, to many spectators without masks who were not socially distancing. The ship had 1,000 hospital beds and 1,200 personnel onboard who were earmarked to treat non-coronavirus patients so the local hospitals could focus on COVID-19 victims. Hope had arrived, and many New Yorkers breathed a collective sigh of relief.

Later that night, we decided to do some research and educate ourselves about homelessness. Joel found a basic fact sheet produced by the Coalition for the Homeless, one of New York City's oldest agencies dedicated to serving the city's homeless population.

According to the agency's website there were 60,422 homeless people in New York, including 13,861 homeless families with 20,494 homeless children sleeping in the city's shelters, an increase of 133 percent since 2010, and the highest statistic on record since the Great Depression. In addition, thousands of other unsheltered homeless people, like the ones we were encountering, slept on the streets or on the subway cars and platforms. While life had been difficult for them before the pandemic, now their survival was all the more threatened.

The fact sheet indicated the primary cause of homelessness among families to be lack of affordable housing, with the major triggering events being eviction, domestic violence, job loss and hazardous housing conditions. In contrast, among single adults, the primary causes were noted as alcohol/drug abuse and mental illness.

The next morning it was raining, and we were tempted to skip our walk. It seemed as though we both had the same idea at the same time, however, because without exchanging words, we put on our coats, grabbed our umbrellas, and set out. When we returned later that afternoon, neither of us had one. There were others who needed them more.

As we walked into our apartment, I looked at my phone and read some good news. Mayor de Blasio had just announced that beginning on Friday, April 3, New York City was expanding its free meal service at schools to include all New Yorkers, regardless of whether they had children. Nevertheless, the free meals were only available Monday through Friday, leaving the hungry to scramble for food on the weekends. It was better than no meals, however.

While my morning walks and efforts to help the homeless induced an inward humanitarian focus, my legal work in the afternoon continued to connect me to the business world. I zigzagged between the two opposing realities.

A battle for where to invest my brain, if not my soul, had begun.

Battle or not, we continued walking. Keeping our distance, we skittered by them, content to be handing out a few dollars here and there. I think we might have even felt a little proud, as much for not giving into the fear of the virus as for the money we shared. We also owned the guilt we felt as we wondered couldn't society do a better job for the homeless? Couldn't we?

Then one day, I stopped to really look at Maggie, the woman who lived on Park Avenue and 30th Street as she busily swept the sidewalk. Later that afternoon, I found myself thinking about her while trying to concentrate on work. The next morning, I set out with the intention of finding her.

As we approached 30th street, Maggie was nowhere to be seen. However, we met the middle-aged man who appeared to be her partner on the same corner. Joel offered him a few dollars, which he accepted with a surprised expression and grateful smile.

"Thank you. My name is Rick."

"I'm Joel, and this is Traci."

"Can I have a dollar for Maggie, please?"

"Who is Maggie?" Joel asked.

"My wife."

"Where is she?"

"She went to look for something to eat."

Joel and I were hesitant to give Rick more money, but we thought Maggie might be the same woman I'd connected with the day before. Joel handed him another few dollars.

I saw Maggie again the next day. She was sleeping on her makeshift bed, snuggled into Rick's arms. I hesitated as I walked by, torn between the opposing desires to give her money and not to disturb her. I'd already learned that sleep did not come easily to the homeless—one eye open, one ear listening, their intermittent rest akin to sentry duty.

Sensing my presence, Maggie stirred and opened her eyes. Her hazy gaze landed directly on me and she smiled faintly when she recognized me. I quietly approached and handed her a few dollars.

The money quickly disappeared up her sleeve as she closed her eyes to return to sleep.

The following day, Maggie and I spoke for the first time.

"Do you know why the money is so important to us?" she asked.

"To buy food?"

"Well, that too, except we can get food at the drop-in center near here—or at the school—even though it's not very good."

"Well, what else is the money used for then?" I asked, fearing her response might be to buy alcohol or drugs.

"To use the bathroom at McDonald's," she replied.

"You have to pay to use the bathroom?"

"Not exactly. You have to buy something to be able to use it, but even a cup of coffee or tea is enough."

During the pandemic the only public bathroom available in the area was at McDonald's on Park Avenue and 28th Street. So small amounts of money represented not just sustenance, but self-respect. Sleeping on the street, panhandling for money, wearing dirty clothes, all appeared tolerable. However, for the most part, relieving oneself on the street was avoided whenever possible.

"So, what's a drop-in center? I continued. "Is that a shelter?"

"Oh, no, we don't go to the shelters."

"Why?"

"We're safer on the streets."

"Wow, really?

"Yep, people are always stealing your things in the shelters. The first night I spent in a shelter was a disaster. I woke up the next morning and my wallet was gone."

"Can't you lock up your things?" I asked.

"Sometimes people steal from the lockers, so we just sleep with our money in our pockets."

"I'm so sorry. I've heard about shelters not being safe, but I didn't realize things could be stolen, too."

"That's why so many of us end up on the streets."

"Well, what's a drop-in center, then?" I repeated.

"A place where you can sleep for a night when it's really cold. It's first-come, first-served though, and they only have chairs to sleep in, not beds. At least you can sleep with your things on your lap, so they're usually safe unless you're really drunk and end up passing out."

"I guess there is a silver lining to everything," I said, in an effort to lighten the mood.

Over the next few days we got to know Maggie and Rick a little better. Maggie told us that they were distantly related, as well as romantic partners, and had known each other since childhood. She told us that Rick had been the result of an affair between his father, a Jewish dentist, and his father's Hispanic dental assistant. He'd grown up in two very different worlds, shuttling back and forth between Brooklyn and New Jersey, not fully belonging in either place. The constant moving was upsetting, and he'd started having emotional outbursts as a young child.

Rick told us the same story about his parents. He added that he'd been homeless for ten years after losing his job as a dental assistant in the 2008 economic downturn. He'd run through two bad marriages and his maximum allowable unemployment benefits before being evicted.

"Why didn't you go live with your mother or father?" Joel asked.

"I was no longer welcome," Rick confessed.

"Why?" Joel probed further.

"I'm an alcoholic. No one wants a drunk around."

Rick began his homelessness in the Bellevue shelter. However, due to fights with other residents, he was told to leave. He then bounced from shelter to shelter, always being thrown out for fighting. Rick was eventually taken in by an elderly woman. When she jumped off the roof of the building they were living in, Rick was homeless again.

After that, another agency that serve the homeless placed him in one of their transitional supportive housing facilities. He lost that room, too, due to fights. After so much turmoil, Rick decided to take his chances on the street, and to his surprise, he liked it.

"It's cold and I'm often hungry," he said. "But I'm always free."

"So, you don't want to be sheltered?" I asked, surprised.

"I wouldn't mind a single room, but I do not ever want to live in a shelter again."

"Because of the rules?"

"Those, too, but mostly because I don't feel safe there."

Rick considered himself a "line walker," a panhandler who approaches cars stopped at a red light. Before the pandemic, he made decent money, sixty to eighty dollars a day, on average. On a really good day, he could make $200. With no expenses, Rick managed to make a living for Maggie and himself until the virus arrived.

"When COVID hit, everything fell apart. For the first time since I'd learned how to make money as a line walker, there were no cars to beg from. There were always cars 24/7. This was the city that never slept. But not a creature was stirring after the virus hit, and it is very scary."

"How much money can you make now?" I asked.

"Virtually nothing."

Maggie told us she was the daughter of two Jewish professionals who had retired to Florida after long and successful careers as teachers. Born into a good family and raised in Brooklyn, Maggie said she'd been given every opportunity to succeed. She was surprised to learn that I'd grown up in Virginia under modest living conditions.

"I thought you were some kind of Connecticut trust-fund baby," she said and laughed.

"No trust funds here, but I was given a good education and that is a blessing that can make a big difference in life."

"It sure can," she agreed. "I went to college too."

I wondered why a college-educated woman would end up homeless, but I decided not to ask her more about it that morning.

Maggie admitted to making many bad choices in her life, most notably related to men. "I have an uncanny knack of finding losers."

"Just about every woman I know, including myself, has a few war stories to share when it comes to men," I admitted.

"My first boyfriend was actually the security guard at my high school," Maggie added. "He was ten years older than me and extremely handsome. He had a car, and I had a complete and total crush on him. Problem was, he returned the interest. Looking back, we were not exactly discreet. We went bowling on Friday nights. We ate at the local diner, and he would drop my friends off at the end of the night. It was completely bizarre, horribly inappropriate, and prompted a lot of lying to my mother.

She knew something was up because he would randomly show up at our house. After about six months, someone must have said something, because one morning, out of the blue, he told me he'd left his job and was moving to Pennsylvania. I'm pretty sure he was fired for inappropriate behavior, but I never asked."

"Well, that was just a high school fling," I said in an effort to maintain our connection.

"True, but it gets worse from there. My tendency to make poor choices followed me to college. That's when I met David and the real trouble began. He was actually my best friend's husband. I had a relationship with him behind her back. Needless to say, after she found out, she never spoke to me again. I don't blame her."

Maggie's bad judgment with men saw a brief reprieve when she married a man from New Jersey who she said got a near-perfect score on his SATs. They had two children and were living with her husband's parents.

"We were happy for a few years even though the relationship was devoid of passion," she admitted. "Then I had an emergency root canal. I was addicted after my first prescription of Percocet."

When Maggie tried to get off the drugs, she started drinking and was frequently drunk. "I have to give her credit," Maggie admitted. "I was drunk and picked a fight with her. She listened to everything I had to say. And then she calmly suggested it would be better for all of us if I moved out."

Maggie told me she asked her husband to leave with her, reasoning that they could afford to rent their own place. He declined.

"Why wouldn't he go with you?" I asked, suspicious that I was not being told the whole story.

"He didn't say, but I don't blame anyone except myself. I was an addict and a drunk. And I'd lost my job because of it. I was just a drain on everyone and needed to get myself together."

"Understood," I said. "But why wouldn't your husband help you find a new place?" I asked.

"He told me to just go spend the night in a hotel and that things would calm down in the morning, and then we'd figure it."

"And were they?"

"No, it only got worse. My drinking escalated, I ran out of money, and before I knew it, my options were few."

"Did you ask to go back?"

"No. I was too proud."

"So then what did you do?"

"My mom helped me get an apartment nearby, and things were okay for a while. A few months later, I lost the apartment."

"Why?"

"Rick was actually living with me at the time. I'd found him in New York and asked him to move to New Jersey. Bad move. One night he got drunk and destroyed the apartment. The next day the landlord kicked us out."

Maggie spent her first night as a homeless woman in a nearby shelter. After her wallet was stolen, she left the following morning. She and Rick lived under the Ferris wheel on the beach in Atlantic City for a few months. When it got cold, they headed to New York City.

"He's the only reason I'm here," she said.

"Can't you both get placed in a room together?" I asked.

"No, because we're not married."

"Oh, yeah, that makes sense," I replied. "Can you maybe get a divorce and then marry Rick?"

"That might work, but I'm afraid unless I get some form of visitation rights, I will never see my children again."

I was getting cold standing on the street corner and motioned to Joel, who was talking to Rick, that it was time to leave. We headed down Park Avenue passing by the middle-aged Black man who we routinely saw sitting in the abandoned telephone booth. He was large. I guessed he was well over two hundred and fifty pounds. His legs appeared swollen, especially his feet, which no longer fit into his shoes. Sometimes a young woman sat in the telephone booth next to him. That day he was alone.

As I dropped some money into his cup, he replied with his customary, "much appreciated."

Joel stopped to talk with him. "How you doing? Do you need anything?"

The man seemed perplexed at Joel's question and shook his head. "I'm okay, I'm okay," he repeated as he gazed off in the distance.

"Well, let us know if you need anything. I'm Joel and this is my wife, Traci."

"Thank you. I'm Bob," he replied.

As we walked back to our apartment I kept thinking what Bob had said. How was it possible that he believed he was okay? Homeless, hungry, and clearly physically challenged, he nevertheless emanated a serenity that I rarely felt in myself.

◆ ◆ ◆

I was surprised when the woman returned two days later. I was sleeping. When I opened my eyes and saw her, there was a gentleness to her that I had not noticed before. I could tell she did not want to wake me, and I appreciated the gesture. I accepted the money gratefully. As I closed my eyes and drifted back to sleep, I found myself hoping she would return again, so that I could properly introduce myself.

I was given the opportunity to do just that when she came back the following day.

"My name is Maggie."

"I'm Traci," she replied with a smile. We didn't shake hands, though. Everyone was afraid to touch anyone because of the virus.

As the days went by, I found myself shocked at how easily I was able to bare my soul to this stranger. I told her things I'd not told anyone since I'd been on the street. She never seemed to judge me and always made light of whatever I "confessed" to her.

I'd become guarded of my identity since becoming homeless, afraid of people finding out just how far I'd fallen. But there I was, opening up to this stranger, not only telling her about what it was like to be homeless, but telling her what it was like to be me.

And she was listening.

But I was hiding secrets from her, and this scared me. Somehow, I just knew she would find out.

Maggie Wright, April 2020

A free ebook edition is available with the purchase of this book.

To claim your free ebook edition:

1. Visit MorganJamesBOGO.com
2. Sign your name CLEARLY in the space
3. Complete the form and submit a photo of the entire copyright page
4. You or your friend can download the ebook to your preferred device

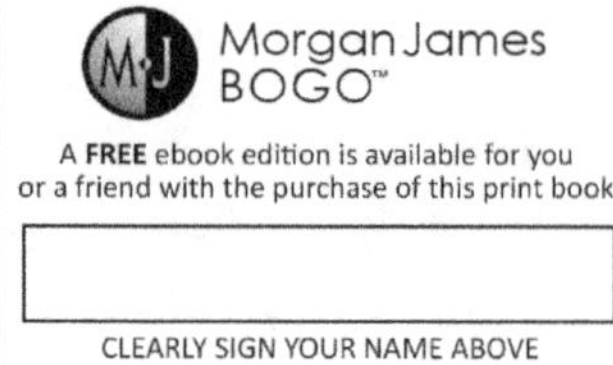

Print & Digital Together Forever.

Snap a photo

Free ebook

Read anywhere

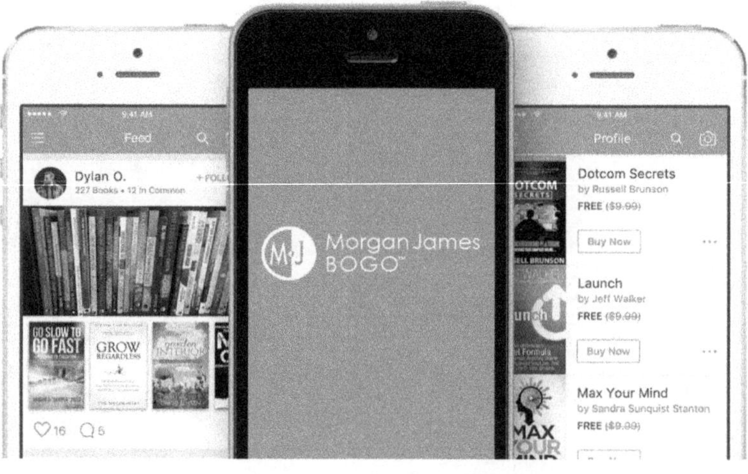

www.ingramcontent.com/pod-product-compliance
Lightning Source LLC
Jackson TN
JSHW081934170226
98182JS00013B/501